ADVANCE PRAISE

"Customer success is a complex and fairly new discipline, but for SaaS companies that want to build an organization (and service) that lasts, it is critical. In his book, The Seven Pillars of Customer Success, Wayne explains the tools every customer success manager needs to have in their toolbox and how to use them throughout the entire customer journey. Witty, clever, and sharp, Wayne explains the customer success function so clearly that even someone with little to no customer success experience will be able to understand it. Everyone in customer success should read this book."

—NICK MEHTA, CEO AT GAINSIGHT

"Wayne has created an easy-to-follow framework for deploying key customer success principles. Just one pillar from this book can make a big impact on your organization. Now imagine all seven combined! There's even a secret bonus Pillar in the book to help attain greater results. This is an excellent read for anyone in CS leadership, anyone who wants to be a CS leader, and any CxO looking for best practices in creating success for their customers."

—MARY POPPEN, CHIEF CUSTOMER
OFFICER, GLINT AT LINKEDIN

"From someone who has been in the customer success profession for over fifteen years, I can truly say this book is a must-read for customer success professionals. Wayne clearly lays out building blocks for a successful CS strategy. He also introduces new concepts, such as a customer churn journey map. I highly recommend it."

—CHAD HORENFELDT, DIRECTOR, CUSTOMER
SUCCESS AT KUSTOMER

"As you read this book, you'll be drawn to action—The Seven Pillars of Customer Success isn't meant to sit on the shelf, but rather be enacted. I'm inspired by Wayne's ability to draw customer success concepts into actionable concepts that can help to transform your customer success practices."

—JEFF BREUNSBACH, DIRECTOR, CUSTOMER
EXPERIENCE AT HIGHER LOGIC

"If you know Wayne, it's easy to understand why he's a Top 100 Customer Success Strategist, as voted by the success community. The Seven Pillars of Customer Success showcases why he holds this title."

—KRISTI FALTORUSSO, VICE PRESIDENT OF
CUSTOMER SUCCESS AT INTLLISHIFT

"Having known Wayne for more than twenty years, I can attest to why he is a Top 100 Customer Success Strategist. In The Seven Pillars of Customer Success, he shares a framework that's easy to follow, implement, and customize for your situation—a culmination of his successful, twenty-five years of experience."

—XINA SEATON, VICE PRESIDENT, CUSTOMER
EXPERIENCE AT BLUE PRISM

"In an industry that is still evolving and increasingly viewed as a growth driver, Wayne has taken the courageous step of distilling a vast amount of information into a repeatable framework. The Seven Pillars of Customer Success is an excellent overview of how to roll out and execute your customer success strategy."

—MATT COLLIER, SENIOR DIRECTOR AT ADOBE

THE
SEVEN
PILLARS
OF
CUSTOMER
SUCCESS

A Proven Framework to Drive Impactful

Client Outcomes for Your Company

WAYNE McCULLOCH

LIONCREST
PUBLISHING

THE SEVEN PILLARS OF CUSTOMER SUCCESS
A Proven Framework to Drive Impactful
Client Outcomes for Your Company

ISBN   978-1-5445-1661-5 *Hardcover*
       978-1-5445-1660-8 *Paperback*
       978-1-5445-1659-2 *Ebook*
       978-1-5445-1662-2 *Audiobook*

For Kristi, who made this—and much more—possible.

CONTENTS

FOREWORD

Wayne McCulloch is one of the most thoughtful customer success leaders I've ever met.

I met Wayne when he was with Looker, a business intelligence company headquartered in Santa Cruz, California. At the time, customer success was top of mind for Looker. Most large-scale software companies evolve to a stage when reinforcing the strength of the existing customer base is paramount. Wayne was a part of that transition at Salesforce and oversaw it at Looker.

I'm a venture capitalist at Redpoint Ventures, which means I partner with early-stage software companies, sometimes when their workforce consists of only a few people, and help them grow by giving them capital and perspective. Redpoint partnered with Looker when the company had 16 employees and worked with the management team to complete its ultimate sale to Google about six years later for $2.7 billion.

In the early days of a company, the most important discipline is product development—the startup needs to make the item it will sell. Once the product is complete enough to sell, the focus of the business swings to building the sales and marketing teams to close new customers. As the company blossoms to hundreds of employees, and tens or hundreds of millions in revenue, retaining and growing customers becomes critical.

Why is this? Imagine your business generates $5 million in revenue this year, and it's growing 300% per year. Next year, the company will book $10 million in new customers and renew approximately $5 million in existing customers. In this scenario, sales has a bigger book of business than customer success.

Fast-forward to when the company records $100 million in revenue and grows at 60% per year. Sales will book $60 million in revenue, while the customer success team renews $100 million.

Every modern software company transitions this way. And there are more and more of them. Our internal analysis shows companies spend about $1.5 trillion per year on software and infrastructure. Only about 20% of that is cloud spend as of this writing. And that 20% has created massive businesses like Salesforce, Zoom, Snowflake, and many others. Along the way, these businesses have created more than $2.5 trillion in market capitalization.

But the cloud won't stop at 20% market penetration. Maybe the cloud captures 60% of the market. That means there's approximately another $5 trillion of market capitalization yet to be shifted and created. That's another 20 Salesforces, or 25 Zooms and 25 Snowflakes. Each of those companies must retain and expand their customers' spend to be successful.

Wayne has seen how customer success operates at the largest SaaS company in history: Salesforce. And he's led the function at one of the fastest-growing business intelligence companies: Looker.

In this book, you'll find a distillation of how he and his teams have accomplished the goal of managing and growing massive customer bases for great companies.

The Seven Pillars of Customer Success is a manual for heads of customer success teams (or divisions) on how to run those teams, whether they are very young or very much at scale.

For each of the seven pillars that Wayne enumerates, he defines concepts, metrics, and tools simply—in ways customer success leaders can immediately apply with their teams.

This book will help customer success leaders in three key ways:

1. Understand the discipline: Leaders will discover customer success best practices in an easy and readily understandable way. They will be introduced to standard customer success tools and learn how to incorporate them in each customer success pillar.
2. Champion the budget necessary to staff the customer success team: Leaders will uncover how to advocate, at the board level, why the customer success function is strategic to the business. This will help them acquire the financing they need to initiate, continue, or increase their company's customer success investment.
3. Recruit and manage the customer success team: Once leaders understand the customer success discipline and have the funds to recruit new talent, they will be better equipped to hire and run a successful team. They will learn what to look for when they recruit and how to support and then scale their teams effectively.

When customers get the most value out of the products they buy, they're happy. When customers are really happy, they spend more. It's that simple.

Customer success is a modern software company's people, policies, and practices used to satisfy and delight customers at scale. To succeed, it's a critical discipline that must be developed. This book is a step-by-step journey to understand and master this crucial subject.

—TOMASZ TUNGUZ

INTRODUCTION

CUT THROUGH THE NOISE

Business leaders everywhere are struggling to understand how to build a sophisticated customer success organization and implement it into their businesses. Did you know there are at least eight different certifications you can receive for customer success? Eight! If I want to become certified in accounting, I become a Certified Public Accountant (CPA). There is *one* certification to become a CPA, so why are eight certifications needed to become a customer success manager (and even more in the future, no doubt)?

Customer success hasn't been around long enough to have well-established standards, which is typical of any new business function still trying to work out its identity. Because customer success is changing and morphing (even as you read this), most people understand it differently or believe it is something it isn't.

In a given year, there are more than 85 customer success conferences around the world and more than 30 different customer success organizations you can join—not to mention the myriad articles, blogs, webinars, and consultancies focused on the topic.

There is so much noise out there that it's hard to sift through the sand and find little nuggets of gold. There are a lot of people who give great advice, but sometimes it's too high level to be actionable or just isn't applicable to your situation.

Needless to say, people are confused. They're reading everything available but are still struggling to understand customer success well enough to build an effective and impactful organization centered on it. They'll follow the opinion of one vendor and, when that doesn't work, pivot to the opinion of another. But these opinions don't show you how to *build* a customer success organization.

Nine times out of ten, the content you're reading was meant to push a specific product or service in the customer success marketplace or simply reflect the narrow personal experiences of the author that may or may not help you. The content wasn't meant to *actually teach you* how to implement customer success—it's usually more about specific tactical aspects of customer success that have worked in specific environments. These books and articles have a lot of useful information in them (and I've learned quite a bit from them myself), but structurally, they aren't very helpful to put into coordinated action. There are great little tidbits throughout, but there is no cohesive way to consume them. They are too scattered and too disorganized.

Ideas are great in theory, but without a framework, how do we implement them? How do we realize those ideas and make them tangible? Reading an article about what to do is an idea that exists without any support around it.

The problem is, the more and more you bite off and chew, the harder the information is to swallow. The more insights you read, the tougher it is to put together a cohesive strategy to build a customer success organization that drives impact for the client. This is the challenge we're seeing today (believe me, I went through this when I started in the customer success world), but it's possible for anyone in customer success to jump in and start building something of value. I'm writing this book to make sense of the current ingredient list and put together a simple recipe that's easy for everyone to follow.

I want to cut through all the noise and genuinely help customer success leaders and managers (current and future) understand customer success. There's a lot of material out there telling you about the history of customer success, but that doesn't help you plan your customer success future. I don't want to waste your time, so I created a framework that makes it easy to understand how to construct an excellent customer success organization.

PRESCRIPTIVE, FLEXIBLE, AND EASY TO USE

First, let me be clear about what this book won't tell you.

It doesn't tell you about the birth of customer success or how customer success came into being. It doesn't tell you about the age of the customer or how SaaS and cloud changed the business model paradigm. It doesn't talk about how customer success managers (CSMs) are the fastest-growing profession on the planet, and it doesn't refer to hundreds of different books, blogs, and white papers (and dozens of other pieces of information), easily searchable on the web.

If that's why you're here, you should put this book down. No, seriously. Put it down—now.

I'm here to help you build an impactful customer success organization because that's what you want, right?

My assumption is you're already well read and are a leader in the customer success space (or soon will be). Yet no matter how much you've read or heard, you're still trying to figure out how to piece together all of the opinions, statistics, and insights (and examples and information and knowledge) you've acquired; you are still struggling to build a world-class organization that drives impactful client outcomes for your company. You picked up *this* book because you're looking for a simple way to do it.

I'm here to tell you, you aren't alone. You aren't the only one stranded on a remote island; almost every customer success professional I've talked to is sending out an SOS signal, too.

This book delivers a prescriptive, flexible, and easy-to-use framework that leaders and future leaders in the customer success function can use to build an excellent customer service organization.

WHAT CUSTOMER SUCCESS CAN LOOK LIKE

My professional life in software began in B2B (business to business) back in the 1990s when I joined a US-based company while living in Melbourne, Australia, called PeopleSoft. To this day, PeopleSoft was one of the best companies I've ever worked for because it had an incredible company culture. (I would add Looker to that list as well.) I worked for them 25 years ago, and some of the people I worked with still get together for happy hours once a month. The culture was *that* impactful.

My chosen field was the training and certification of customers and partners, which was the perfect place for me to start my customer success journey. The ability to get a customer to adopt your software is one of the most preeminent components of retention, expansion, and advocacy; through training and certifications, software adoption was the main function of my job.

While I was at PeopleSoft, customer success didn't exist yet because the SaaS and cloud models hadn't yet been delivered to the market. It took those two tech paradigm changes to drive the invention of a dedicated customer success function. My formal introduction to the world of customer success officially began inside Salesforce.

A WONDER TO BEHOLD

Salesforce is known as the pioneer of customer success, and when I walked into Salesforce on my first day (many years ago), their customer success organization was a true wonder to behold. Most impressively, they had a data science team who focused solely on customer success.

Early on, Salesforce understood that data would help drive the best decisions, so their team of data scientists built an algorithm called EWS (early warning system) that factored in over 120 different inputs to calculate a customer health score. At a super-high confidence level, this score predicted customer churn nine months in advance giving their customer success team enough time to change the paradigm and retain their customers. It also predicted potential problems, triggered notifications to the right people, and delivered playbooks of proven best practices in order to solve those problems.

Imagine that level of sophistication. Most companies I talk to today don't even have a playbook. They don't have a health score or a team of data scientists. They sort of "wing it." When a customer says they're leaving, they get reactive and it's all hands on deck. This is very different than Salesforce, which can predict and prescribe what needs to be done to keep the customer, well in advance of the potential problem. As customer success leaders, we should aim for the level of sophistication we see at Salesforce.

Salesforce is a juggernaut in the software industry; 20 years in, its growth continues to be stellar, and in every major city, there's a massive commercial building with the Salesforce logo at the very top.

While I was there, I got to work with one of the world's most accomplished customer success leaders, Maria Martinez. At Salesforce, she pioneered an impactful customer success culture that drove the overall prosperity of the company. I am very fortunate and honored to have worked under her and been a part of the customer success function while she was there; my experience with Salesforce helped me understand, at scale, what customer success can truly look like.

After Salesforce, I took a role as a Chief Customer Officer, which gave insight into how customer-facing functions operated. This included areas such as support, training, renewals, *and* customer success. I got to see how all those functions worked together to create great customer experiences that led to retention, expansion, and advocacy. This gave me a fantastic advantage; I learned how customers viewed great customer experience.

I also learned that customer success was much broader than the customer success function itself, because I managed all the internal teams responsible for enabling a successful customer. I learned where customer success needed to integrate and share metrics with other functions within the company to amplify its ability to be effective, impactful, and successful. I learned that customer success was truly a methodology that carried across every company department. Later, I went to a similar role at Looker, where I was able to build on that body of knowledge.

Today, I'm lucky to have a customer success leadership role at Google. My current experience specializing in customer success has further increased my ability to understand how all of these internal functions are able to work in different environments. I've worked for small companies and large companies, public and private, and I've seen how rigid instructions or direction when building a customer success organization is actually *not* helpful. Customer success is always changing and morphing based on the business needs around it, so the tools we use to manage it need to be flexible. They can't be static.

THE SEVEN PILLARS OF CUSTOMER SUCCESS

The Seven Pillars of Customer Success is a framework designed to show you how to create and execute a sophisticated and impactful customer success organization, regardless of company maturity or industry.

In the first part of the book, I'm going to run through the ten tools every customer success professional needs in their arsenal:

- Moments of Truth
- Playbooks

- Customer Health
- Customer Risk Framework
- Customer Success Plans
- Segmentation
- Voice of the Customer
- QBRs and EBRs
- Customer Delight
- Metrics

Once we nail that down (there's a quiz at the end—just kidding!), I focus on the seven pillars in Part 2:

- Pillar #1: Operationalizing Customer Success
- Pillar #2: Onboarding
- Pillar #3: Adoption
- Pillar #4: Retention
- Pillar #5: Expansion
- Pillar #6: Advocacy
- Pillar #7: Strategic Advisor

I'm giving you the blueprints to build your customer success house, but how you design and decorate that house (and whether you decide to splurge on an 80" flat-screen TV) is completely up to you. I want to genuinely help you build your customer success house. I'm not here to preach and I'm not here to sell you on specific fixtures.

The framework will work for a variety of metrics and a variety of businesses because that's how they were designed. You will always be able to augment the pillars and add external knowledge and skills based on your own personal experience. Once you build out your customer success organization, you can invent your own best practices based on your unique industry and what you're seeing in the market.

If you can say what your company focuses on, how you deliver value, and how you measure success, your customers are clear on what you do. You've established yourself and the problem your company is out there to solve. But as you take on customers and work to solve that problem, you realize customer success is *the only function* that stays with the customers through all stages of their journey with the company.

When you think about it, the functional name "customer success" is a little frustrating in itself because it insinuates that the people who work in customer success are solely focused on the customer, but customer success is there to help all departments better serve the customer along their journey. Sales comes in, sells, and moves on to another customer. Services comes in and implements, but once the implementation or project is done, they leave, too. Support is there when the customer needs you, but they aren't there when you don't immediately need them. Customer success is the one constant in the customer's life cycle with your company (well, it should be if it isn't).

Customer success is *always* there (physically or digitally), and this philosophy should be spread out across the entire company. It isn't just a little department that only owns the success of the customer; it is essential for the success of all departments. The reality of the situation is that you have to build a culture of customer success inside your organization because to be successful, you have to teach your peers how to utilize it.

IT'S HARD TO TAKE THE FIRST STEP

The hardest part of any journey is the first step, and I'm trying to make it as easy as possible for customer success professionals to be successful. This book is a one-stop shop for anyone who wants to build an excellent customer success organization.

Right now, there is no real definitive standard for customer success, and until there is one, there is going to be confusion. I'm giving you the framework and the ability to construct and navigate your customer success organization regardless of what's going on around you. *The Seven Pillars of Customer Success* will help filter out the noise, the latest trends, and the newest influencer sharing ideas or concepts that might not make sense for your company, your product, or your industry.

The beauty of the Seven Pillars of Customer Success is that it is flexible enough to help any type of business and will also help you scale. Whether you're a small, $5 million startup, a midsize company getting ready to scale, or a multibillion-dollar enterprise, the framework allows you to build an executable strategy because that's what's going to be useful to you, no matter where you are in your business.

My aim in this book is to give you a very unbiased view of what I have known to be successful in delivering a great customer success organization. I also aim to give you something that is timeless. I felt compelled to write this book because I realized the Seven Pillars of Customer Success is the same framework our predecessors were using 20 years ago. Sure, I may have organized them and given them names, but the pillars are the same now as they were back then. What happens inside each pillar will change based on the needs of the business, but the pillars themselves haven't changed in many decades because it's based on people, not technology or trends.

Noise doesn't matter. What matters is this framework. Regardless of your budget or company size, *The Seven Pillars of Customer Success* will allow you to build an effective customer success organization that will deliver impactful client outcomes for your company. In the first part of the book, I'm going to bring us all onto the same page. I'm going to talk about the language of customer success and introduce the tools that will be used throughout this book. Then, in the second part, I'll take you through the seven pillars.

PART ONE

═══

LANGUAGE AND TOOLS

CHAPTER 1

THE LANGUAGE OF CUSTOMER SUCCESS

I was a latchkey kid. I had a single mom, and we were living at the poverty line. By the time I was six, I was skipping school regularly, and for the next two years, I hung out with other kids who were in similar situations. We would get into all sorts of trouble, such as break into houses and steal car radios; it wasn't long before I had a run-in with the police. The next thing I knew, my grandparents stepped in. They had recently retired from the police force and lived on a farm. They loved farming life and thought it would do me, a rough city kid, some good.

When I first got there, my grandparents thought it would help me adjust if they taught me some basic bush survival skills. We lived in an isolated environment, surrounded by a state forest, and they thought it was vital that I knew these skills in case I were to ever need them in the future. If I got lost, for example, would I know how to make it back to the farm? If they drove me out into the middle of the bush, gave me a compass, a map, and a canteen of water, would I be able to find my way home?

My grandparents were teaching me the skills to survive in the bush, but it was also a metaphor: they were giving me the skills to be self-sufficient when things went wrong.

In customer success, we want our customer success team to be self-sufficient. When things are bleak, we want them to be able to navigate to a better place. We want them armed with the ability to find their way home—all to create the best experience for the customer. The customer success language and tools give our customer success team those skills.

CUSTOMER SUCCESS IS RESPONSIBLE FOR...

As mentioned in the Introduction, there's a lot of noise about what customer success is, who does it, and how it's done. I want to get us on the same page with some foundational ideas and terms that I'll use throughout the book.

Customer success has five main responsibilities:

1. Eliminate churn through value attainment
2. Drive increased contract value through value expansion
3. Improve the customer experience
4. Gain customer acquisition through building advocacy
5. Proactively lead the customer (to success)

Let's look at each one.

ELIMINATE CHURN THROUGH VALUE ATTAINMENT

There are two different types of churn. Logo churn happens when the customer leaves and doesn't renew. Let's say you have a Netflix subscription, but you decide to drop Netflix and switch to Hulu because it has a better selection or costs less. That's logo churn, leaving one brand for another.

Revenue churn occurs when the customer stays but pays you less. You might be a subscriber to Netflix Premium but wake up one day and say, "You know, I'm not using it that much, so I'm going to change my subscription to pay less." You're not switching brands; you're just downsizing. That's revenue churn, and CSMs are responsible for managing both.

Revenue churn can happen because the customer no longer finds your product or service valuable. It can also occur when they haven't used up all their licenses and renew for less. Sometimes it's even a little bit of both.

INCREASE PROFITABILITY

What happens when we reduce churn? Profits increase.

Customer lifetime value (CTV) is a metric that measures customer profitability. It's what makes companies like Salesforce extremely valuable. The SaaS company is worth around $200 billion but is earning only just over $20 billion in annual revenue. It is valued at such high multiples because it has a future revenue stream; customers are locked in for two, three, four, or more years. They have contractually obligated, consistent revenue from existing customers.

When you acquire a new customer, it costs a lot of money. First, you have to fund your marketing department, and then you have to buy advertising, attend conferences and trade shows, and demonstrate a proof of concept. You also have to develop and host a website with a great customer user experience and SEO (search engine optimization) and SEM (search engine marketing) built-in.

And those are just the costs to promote your brand and generate awareness. You also need to pay for the people who are going to prospect for customers and more people who are going to convince them to do business with you (field sales, presales, solution specialists, etc.). Once you do, additional people in legal and finance are needed to settle the terms and complete the transaction. All those expenses certainly add up!

Organizations spend more money to acquire new customers than they do to keep existing ones, so to be as profitable as possible, we need to retain customers. That also means, the longer we retain them, the more profit they generate.

In my experience, the breakeven point for a customer to start generating a profit is typically around the 18-month mark. This varies depending on industry, product type, and company maturity, but I have found that if a company churns a customer within the first 18 months, the company will typically lose money. On the other hand, if you keep a customer for five years, everything past month 18 is "practically" pure profit.

Customer retention is one of the simplest ways to achieve profitability, ergo customer success can drive company profits.

DRIVE INCREASED CONTRACT VALUE THROUGH VALUE EXPANSION

Each customer has a chunk of money to spend on technology, IT, and software, and our goal is to maximize how much they spend with us. That doesn't mean we're always selling the customer; the purpose of maximizing contract value is to deliver additional value to the customer. Driving business outcomes is all that matters and the more value we can drive for the customer, the more money they're willing to spend with us (value expansion). Unlike the sales team that is driven by a quota, customer success is driven by value, and the better the value, the better the sales team is set up to close new business.

IMPROVE THE CUSTOMER EXPERIENCE

Customer success professionals aren't the owners of every interaction your customer has with your company. But they do have the responsibility to point out other areas of the company that aren't living up to their promises or creating positive moments of truth for the customer.

On the flip side, CSMs are also responsible for telling internal teams when they're doing an amazing job. Customer success professionals aren't just the organization's police force; they're also parents. They call out the good and the bad—and do it from the perspective of the customer.

CUSTOMER ACQUISITION THROUGH BUILDING ADVOCACY

If we can create, find, and nurture advocates inside our customer base, marketing can amplify their voices via blogs, conferences, case studies, and references. Advocates are another asset that sales professionals can leverage to improve their sales process because ultimately, people trust other customers more than they trust you. You think you have the best solution (of course you do!), but your customers aren't necessarily looking for the best. They're looking for a partner that can drive the best outcome, and advocates can communicate that message.

PROACTIVELY LEAD THE CUSTOMER TO SUCCESS

There's no denying customer success was reactive when it was first created—born out of a need to onboard customers, plug product gaps, manage escalations, and deliver an excellent high-touch support experience. However, as engineering, product, and design teams become smarter (in how they deliver their cloud-based SaaS products) and the voice of the customer is more listened to and more relevant than ever, customer success can now pivot toward its major strength—leading customers to success. (A lot more on this later in this book.)

THE CUSTOMER JOURNEY

The customer journey is the full set of experiences the customer will have when interacting with your company or brand.

The customer journey is the entire time the customer spends with you as a vendor. It is a path you have either researched or captured. Five of the seven pillars represent stages that happen along the journey, but they aren't always linear. For example, *expansion* (pillar #5) leads to *onboarding* (pillar #2) a new department within an existing customer's company. These are pillars but are also stages in the customer's journey. Some customers have a dozen onboarding stages along their journey and others, only one.

Most companies have created or captured the customer journey on a customer journey map (which is simply a visual representation of the customer journey you've researched/captured).

Customer Journey Map Example (Simple)

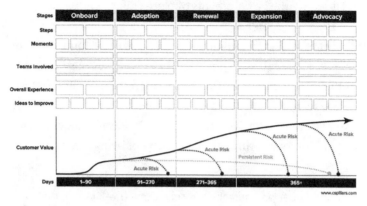

Stages	Onboard		Adoption		Renewal		Expansion		Advocacy	
Steps										
Moments										
Teams Involved										
Overall Experience										
Ideas to Improve										
Customer Value				Acute Risk	Acute Risk Persistent Risk		Acute Risk		Acute Risk	
Days	1–90		91–270		271–365		365+			

Typically, they're developed by marketing departments and focus on the sales and marketing funnel. Marketing's main focus is on converting prospects into customers. Nurture campaigns and lead conversions are well mapped out because, for decades, sales and marketing worked together to understand the customer journey through the sales pipeline.

But these traditional customer journey maps often stop as soon as the prospect becomes a customer. Customer success was the first business function to step up and say, "We need to *own* the journey of the customer *after* the conversion." In today's SaaS and cloud world, we need to understand the customer's entire journey so we know when to intervene, when to help, and when to add value. You can do this visually by creating a customer journey map.

There are many reasons why we must have a customer journey map built, but the most critical are:

1. Accelerate the customer's time to value.
2. Identify efficiencies, such as where you can automate parts of the journey or eliminate steps in the journey that aren't needed or slow down value attainment.

3. Identify the key moments of truth (more on this later).

There are at least 50 million different types of customer journey maps that exist. If you google "customer journey map" and look at the images, you'll see they're all different. Some are sophisticated, some are a little crazy, and some are simple. Some were even written on the back of a napkin! It doesn't matter as long as you've thought through the process of being a customer.

> The number one mistake I've seen done (I've done it, too) is to create a customer journey map based on *the vendor's* own viewpoint of the customer.

"The customer's going to buy our product, then they're going to deploy our product, and then they're going to use the product."

Companies look at it from the vendor's perspective when they should be looking at it from the perspective of the customer. There are so many other things the customer is doing that the vendor doesn't see and isn't involved in. Creating a customer journey map takes a lot of work. It isn't easy. You have to collect data from your customers and prospects (include them in the discussion) and piece the journey together from their perspectives. It's an extensive process but extremely valuable. And this should be a living document, not a static, one-and-done activity. Journeys change, and we should, too.

When you understand the journey from the customer's perspective, you can relate to their painful experiences and potentially lessen the negative impact because you're aware of the problem ahead of time. By really understanding the customer needs and their pains, you can structure touch points to create effective and efficient processes that will deliver success and a great customer experience. I always recommend creating a customer journey map you're comfortable with before embarking on your Seven Pillars journey.

"A hard truth about customer journey maps is that even though they look nice, the maps don't generate an outcome by themselves. A journey map is a means to an end. The success of a journey map should be judged by what it enables people to create in terms of an improved customer experience."

—PETER THOMSON, DIGITAL BRAND STRATEGIST
BASED IN AUCKLAND, NEW ZEALAND

CHURN JOURNEY MAP

A different type of customer journey map is a churn journey map, and I haven't been able to find anything like it yet. Everyone has a customer journey map—this is the trial, this is how we nurture them, this is how we convert them, this is how we wow them, this is how we expand them—but no one maps out *why customers leave* through a journey map. They will do churn reviews and analysis, but they don't *map* it. I found this simple step provided important clarity and an ideal way to align the cross-functional teams needed to help partner on eliminating churn.

Now, that's thinking outside the map...errr...box!

Once a customer leaves, you have to go back and map out their entire journey. You have to find out what went wrong and what went right. And you have to do this for as many customers that leave so you can look for journey patterns. The patterns are the key.

But you shouldn't do this yourself. I highly recommend you hire a third-party vendor to interview the customers who left. If you conduct the exit interview yourself, you'll probably be told lies because your customer doesn't want to hurt your feelings or thinks you are trying to find a way "back in." They're not going to tell you the truth because you're their vendor. A third party is agnostic and has absolutely no skin in the game. When you bring in a third party, they can discuss every step of the customer's journey with the customer in a much safer environment.

"Tell us about this. Tell us about that. How was this? What did you hate about that?"

When the interviews are done, you can then begin to look for patterns of behaviors, systems, processes, people, and so forth that are inhibiting value and preventing the customer from deriving value from your product. Once you find those patterns, you have your churn journey map.

A churn journey map makes it crystal clear where focus is needed to solve negative customer experiences, and many times, you'll discover a problem you didn't even know existed. In some cases, you'll discover it isn't something you're doing; it's something you're *not* doing. I've created churn journey maps at my last three companies and discovered unbelievable insights.

A customer may struggle, for example, to explain the value of the software you've provided because they're not a business value consultant. They didn't study return on investment (ROI) metrics—that isn't their skillset. Now, imagine you, as the customer success organization, were able to come in and add project benchmarks and create tangible, defensible metrics to help your customer tell that story to their leadership. That would be a massive help, wouldn't it?

In this example, as the vendor, you aren't responsible for why the customer is struggling. You're not doing anything wrong. But without a churn journey map, you're going to miss the fact that some customers need extra help presenting the product internally in order for their management to deem the project successful. A churn journey map shows you where you are failing so you can make improvements, enhance your offering, and reduce churn.

Here's an example:

Customer Churn Journey

Not all customers experience the exact same issues on the customer journey; these are examples of customers impacted at different stages.

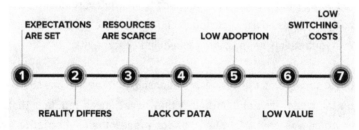

www.cspillars.com

THOUGHT LEADERSHIP SERIES: RON CARSON

*I first met **Ron Carson, Founder and CEO of Thirdside,** at a former company when I needed to understand why customers were leaving. I was looking at the attrition data our field teams had entered into Salesforce and saw things like "Value not attained," "Competitor," "Product fit," and so on. The trouble was, I couldn't act against these reasons. So I asked Ron and his company to reach out to all churned customers to tell me EXACTLY why they left, and he delivered. He helped me to create the churn journey map I use (and advocate for) every chance I can. Take it away, Ron!*

YOUR CUSTOMERS ARE LYING TO YOU: HOW TO MAP THEIR *REAL* CHURN JOURNEY

It's an age-old story, and it happens to nearly every business. A company signs on a new customer and delivers the goods or service. Everyone seems happy during scheduled checkpoints.

But at some point, the business relationship that seemed fine sours—on the customer's end. Although they never raised red flags that anything was wrong, they leave or don't renew their subscription.

If it's ever happened to you, you know that at this point, there is very little hope of recovering the account. In B2B, any number of things could have happened.

Your customer didn't find enough value in your solution to justify the cost.

There was employee turnover, and your champion left.

They found a solution with a competitor.

They were so frustrated—they just wanted to sneak away and never see you again.

The sad thing is that there were likely clear signals that things were awry. The problem is this: you couldn't see them.

Net Promoter Score surveys, technical support, and customer success programs can all miss the warning signs. Your operation reviews and KPIs probably aren't covering every hurdle.

And now that the customer is gone, you'll never be able to uncover the problem.

Or, at least, that's what you think.

In reality, you can find the answers, but you can't do it alone. You need professional help. You need someone they'll never lie to.

You need a third party—someone who will uncover bumps in the customer journey that you never knew existed.

CUSTOMER RENEWALS DIE IN THE DARK

In a time of chatbots and artificial intelligence (AI), we still need to pick up the phone and have an actual conversation with people, talking and asking questions.

Qualitative research conversations provide an unmatched opportunity to uncover blind spots and pull on the threads as they come up. But mapping a customer's journey with internal resources is a challenge. Here's why.

DEVELOPMENT CAN'T DO IT.

What if the reason is a clunky or slow product? Your former customer wants to move along—they definitely *don't* want to tell your development team, "Your baby's ugly." For your employee, even those with the best intentions, pride of ownership can taint the interview.

SALES CAN'T DO IT.

With their bias toward closing, they will, even inadvertently, skew the research results toward the features, messaging, or value proposition that will close the next deal in the pipeline. And don't you really want them focused on closing anyway?

MARKETING CAN'T DO IT.

Marketing often is lower in the political power base pecking order than development, sales, or the C-suite. Issues raised are not always received with the gravity they deserve.

Even if one of your employees does have a seemingly good conversation about your customer's journey, there is a good chance you are going to get all variations of the "it's not you, it's me" theme.

More commonly, unintentional mistakes are being made by your company throughout the actual customer journey that lead to customer churn. Here is an illustrative example:

A sale is made with big promises of what's to come, and presales engineers wow customers with their expertise.

However, the implementation team is made up of B players who don't have the full context of the solution from presales.

A frustrated customer perseveres through the miscommunication and mismatched expectations.

But now the project is overbudget and late.

Given the sensitive nature of the relationship, even good customer service isn't perceived as responsive.

Promised features and enhancements never appear.

The customer begins to find workarounds, and the value of the solution diminishes.

The customer decides months before the contract renewal to leave.

That call from your "success manager" to discuss future needs is pointless, if not borderline offensive.

A THIRD PARTY CAN DO IT

To understand the exact point when your customer decided to walk away and how you can save the next one, you need a third party leading the conversation. Not only are your employees not cut out for the work, but your former customers will also be more candid.

With a third party, customers will be less apprehensive that a sales pitch will be sprung on them or a sales call will "coincidentally" come their way soon.

Similarly, customers will be more likely to talk critically about their experience because they aren't chatting with the person who was the problem—or one of that person's colleagues.

An experienced third party can uncover the actual customer journey—not some mythical odyssey your in-house team pastes into a PowerPoint. You'll learn the good and the bad. And with it, you'll get the actionable insights required to ensure you don't lose any more customers for the same reasons in the future.

A BRIEF HISTORY OF THE CSM

Who, though, does all this work? Let's take a look at the evolution of customer success roles to determine how the work is being done today.

Customer success is involved at every stage of the customer's journey.

I had considered adding another pillar called Preboarding to address the CSM's involvement in the presales cycle but decided to focus on the customer once they have committed to the partnership—otherwise, they are prospects, not customers (or are they?). Once an existing customer, the Expansion Pillar will take care of the preboarding component. (There are differing opinions on this, so I've included a bonus chapter at the end to give you a little more detail on this mysterious pillar.)

A customer success team should consist of, at a minimum, CSMs and CS Ops (customer success operations). We'll spend more time talking about CS Ops personnel a bit later, but the CSM role has evolved through each of the three waves of customer success. So we'll look at the role through the lens of those waves.

THE FIRST WAVE OF CUSTOMER SUCCESS

In the first wave, CSMs were hired to stop churn and focus on retention only. These were the prehistoric days of customer success, in the early 2000s with the birth of SaaS, so there were no processes and no best practices. Because retaining a customer was (and still is) much cheaper than finding a new one, the job of the CSM was to put out fire after fire in order to save the relationship and keep the customer from leaving.

CSMs were first created to solve one problem: eliminate customer churn. That is still a key focus for CSMs today. Customer lifetime value (CLV) is still a valuable business metric, and retaining customers remains the primary focus of all successful customer success organizations.

THE SECOND WAVE OF CUSTOMER SUCCESS

We are currently in the maturing stage of wave two. Originally, customer success was focused solely on retention, but as the customer and marketplace changed, the demand for customer success changed, too. Evolutions in engineering, product, and design teams have done a lot to alleviate the need for human intervention for these reasons.

As customer success got more sophisticated in wave two, we recognized that in order to eliminate churn, we had to show value. We had to prove we were a good partner.

Customer: "Wow, you guys have been invaluable! What else can you do for me?"

CSM: "What about this product? I've seen it used by one of my other customers and they've had a lot of success. Do you want me to set you up with a conversation with our sales team to find out what they can do for you?"

Suddenly, the CSM was thrust into the world of value expansion, looking for and creating qualified leads for the sales team to close. In some cases, those leads even turned into commercial expansion agreements. And once these CSMs added enough value, something else happened—their customers became company advocates and brand ambassadors.

When you provide enough value, you suddenly have customers who are ready and willing to talk about their terrific experience with your company. "Trust these guys; they know what they're doing" or "We've had great success. You're in good hands." Company advocates are what can really skyrocket the success of your business. Word of mouth is one of the most trusted forms of marketing.

Wave one was firefighting retention. In wave two—where we are today—a CSM has responsibilities across onboarding, adoption, retention, expansion, and advocacy. But it won't stay that way.

THE THIRD WAVE OF CUSTOMER SUCCESS

Wave three is coming. It's embracing the seventh pillar and building a customer success team so skilled in their products, their customers' businesses, and their customers' industries that the customer is willing to *pay* for it. As customers grow and become more verticalized, the next wave of customer success teams will be able to provide value and offer services and products to solve complex business problems. They will be able to monetize the next wave of customer success.

Now the most forward-thinking customer success organizations are moving toward the third wave of customer success, where CSMs will drive their own revenue streams through strategic success services.

IS THERE A CUSTOMER SUCCESS PHILOSOPHY?

Most business leaders think having a customer success team automatically makes the customer happy. "We're very customer-centric." "We're customer-focused." "The customer is number one." But a gap exists between their way of thinking and a true company philosophy of customer success. Other teams inside your organization may not realize they're also impacting the customer journey and the value customers derive from the company. Here's a typical example:

> Professional services leader: "Our professional services team is very customer-success focused."
>
> Me: "Awesome. What are the PS team's metrics of success?"
>
> PS leader: "Um, revenue, margin, and utilization."
>
> Me: "Um, okay. Which one of those metrics is about the customer's success?"
>
> PS leader: (blank stare)

Voice of the customer is another good example to review first. For example, you need to be conscious of how often your customers are being surveyed. A few years ago, I was talking to one of my customers and was surprised to learn the number of customer surveys he was receiving from my company.

"We get surveys two times a week or more from your company."

"That doesn't make any sense! We have distribution rules in place to prevent that," I said. I was shocked.

"Yep. The support organization sends out a CSAT survey after every ticket, professional services sends out a checkpoint survey every other week, and the product team sends a survey once a quarter. The marketing department runs a user survey monthly, and the CS team sends out a CS survey before every QBR."

He continued to rattle off what sounded like 100 surveys, which in my opinion, seems like a terrible experience for the customer!

So I asked, "What's the most annoying thing about these surveys? Filling them out?"

"Oh, no," he said. "They're usually short, and I don't mind answering a few questions. It takes only a few minutes, so I'll do a handful of them and ignore others, depending on how busy I am."

"Well, that's good to hear."

"It's nice to know your company is interested in my insight"—he paused—"as long as you acknowledge and act on it. That's the most annoying thing. Taking the time to complete the survey and getting no response or change from a vendor...or even an acknowledgment."

You need to be conscious of how often your customers are being surveyed (and how long those surveys are), but more significantly, you need to pay even closer attention to how their feedback is being recognized and utilized. It's what you do with the feedback that matters.

Why are you surveying them in the first place? Is it for *vanity*? Just to see what they think of you? That's just going to annoy the customer, which will impact their survey responses. They aren't going to answer truthfully if they're irritated. They may not even answer at all!

And if you don't have time to follow up with a customer about their feedback, don't bother. Removing unnecessary surveys (that no one from your company will follow up on because it's simply an internal metric) will make your customer's experience easier and better. Think about the experience from the perspective of your customer and try to make everything as easy as possible.

That's why customer success should be a company philosophy, not limited to a department of people, although the customer success team carries the torch for the philosophy and coordinates customer success activities. We don't want one team to care about customer success; we want the whole company to care.

So how do we make customer success a philosophy and not just a department? We have to help the rest of the company understand their role in making the customer successful. We can encourage the finance team to add little notes to the invoices such as, "We love working with you as a procurement team!" A simple example like this would help make the company more customer-centric.

When your company embraces a customer success philosophy

and each department focuses on enhancing their moments of truth with their customers, you will see a better customer experience and an increased financial return.

How do you get there? By building your seven pillars. To build anything, however, you need to fill your Customer Success Toolbox with the right tools. These next ten mini chapters explain the tools you'll use to build and deliver your seven pillars.

CHAPTER 2

═══

THE CUSTOMER SUCCESS TOOLBOX

Customer success is like the Australian outback—it's wild, untamed, and unmapped. As I mentioned earlier, my grandparents taught me the tools to survive in the Australian bush. They taught me how to read a map and use a compass. They taught me how to conserve energy and resources and how to use a pocketknife ("that's not a knife..."). I even spent three weeks in the bush with nothing but a backpack, a small amount of food, and a bivvy (yep, that's Australian slang right there). My grandparents knew I needed those skills and those tools to survive in the bush, should I get lost. They knew, from experience, I couldn't do it on my own.

Customer success is no different. To build an excellent customer success organization, to really *survive* in the world of customer success, there are a series of tools you will need to scale your best practices in a repeatable way. The Customer Success Toolbox has ten different tools (named T1, T2, T3, etc., for short) to add to your arsenal—weapons you have at your disposal in the battle to survive (and thrive) in the customer success outback.

On the following pages, you'll read about each tool singly, then in Part 2, you'll learn how the tools are used in the seven pillars of the framework. Some of these terms might be familiar to you, but I've provided a full explanation to share how I view and use them for the seven pillars (because, well, it's in a book).

Customer Success Toolbox

T1	Moments of Truth (MOT)	**T6**	Segmentation
T2	Playbooks	**T7**	Voice of the Customer
T3	Customer Health	**T8**	QBRs/EBRs
T4	Customer Risk Framework	**T9**	Customer Delight
T5	Success Plans	**T10**	Metrics

www.cspillars.com

T1: MOMENTS OF TRUTH

The first official tool in our toolbox comes from the book *Moments of Truth*, written by Scandinavian businessman Jan Carlzon. So let's use his definition:

> *Anytime the customer comes into contact with any aspect of a company, however remote, he or she has an opportunity to form an impression.*

Carlzon describes using this concept to turn Scandinavian Airlines into one of the most successful airlines in the industry. When he took over as CEO in the '80s, flights were never on time, and the airline had a bad reputation, but in less than a year, he turned it into a profit machine. And he did it using moments of truth.

Moments of truth are tiny little interactions that happen all the time. They can be digital, they can be offline, and they can be in person. An example of a digital moment of truth would be your website, your documentation, your online chat feature, or even an email a customer receives from you. Even though there is no physical human contact involved, the customer is still interacting with your company, so there's no reason why you shouldn't make that digital interaction a good one.

You can ensure offline experiences are positive, too. Let's say you're sending an invoice to the customer's finance team and you notice the numbers are off. You know it will be painful for the procurement team to research the mistake, but by doing your due diligence and ensuring the invoice is right before it goes out, you're saving your customer the hassle of figuring it out themselves. Live person moments of truth can happen during a phone call, an in-person meeting, or a live event, like a hack-athon. A moment of truth is any touch point your customer has with your company, and these experiences should all be positive.

The Walt Disney Company also understands the importance of moments of truth.

> *"No one owns the customer, but someone always owns the moment."*
>
> —SCOTT HUDGINS, CHIEF COMMERCIAL OFFICER,
> WALT DISNEY WORLD RESORT

In every company, I have seen confusion over who owns the customer. Sales says, "I closed that account; that's mine. You need to talk to me every time you talk to them." And the services team responds, "We're deploying this software right now, so you need to butt out and let us handle the customer." And when something goes wrong, who gets yelled at?

When everyone understands and focuses on owning the moment, rather than the customer, these discrepancies magically disappear.

Hudgins is spot-on, and it's obvious Disney is pretty good at this. Their customer experience is unrivaled because they're clear on who owns the moment. In SaaS and cloud companies, we need to define who owns the moment and to do everything they can to make the experience, these moments of truth, great for the customer.

MOMENTS OF TRUTH TRIGGERS

Moments of truth should be a positive experience for the customer. They should also trigger some kind of interaction between your company and the customer. For example, if the customer calls support, it triggers someone to respond. If someone visits your website and requests a white paper, it triggers the immediate electronic delivery of that white paper.

Moments of truth are seen throughout the customer journey and trigger interaction from all company departments. It's the customer success team's responsibility to understand the company's response to these triggers.

I see five main triggers that exist for moments of truth:

1. **Life-cycle stage triggers** directly connect to the seven pillars. As you move from onboarding to adoption to retention, how do you ensure your customer's experiences are good ones? What are the moments of truth and triggers you should be thinking about?
2. **Customer event triggers** happen when there is a decline in usage, a change in a sponsor, or a low NPS (Net Promoter Score) is reported. Each of these examples requires the CSM to reach out to the customer via email or a phone call or visit.
3. **Scheduled event triggers** are regular monthly check-ins (which

could be an email or a phone call) or regular product renewals (which could entail internal meetings and external sales calls). These triggers can also be regular QBRs and regular EBRs, which are explained in greater detail later.

4. **CSM-defined triggers** are uptelling (more on this term later), cross-telling, and customer webinars. This could mean initiating a marketing campaign or sending out webinar invites.

5. Finally, **vendor-driven triggers** are things such as:

    a. *Release readiness*, where you speak to your customers about the latest release and how to drive more value

    b. *Hackathons*, where you ask new and existing users to try to solve challenges with your solution

    c. *Customer advisory boards* that bring together customers from similar industries or who have similar cohort characteristics (such as the largest, annual recurring revenue) or similar life cycles (new, mature, etc.).

IMPROVE LOYALTY, ONE MOMENT OF TRUTH AT A TIME

Positive moments of truth (like a personalized, positive note from finance) improve the potential for loyalty, which helps extend your customer's lifetime value. This can also drive expansion because loyal customers are likely to buy more given the opportunity. They're also more likely to advocate for your company and potentially become an ambassador, which ultimately results in increased customer recommendations and future sales to new logos.

T2: PLAYBOOKS

Probably my favorite tool, the customer success playbook is a must-have for your company's CS Ops. A playbook tells you how (and when) to respond in an efficient and repeatable way at scale. It includes templates, best practices, strategies, collateral, and more. Organizations like Salesforce or Google have dozens of playbooks covering a broad range of topics. Having playbooks sets the standard for your operating procedures and allows you to train new hires quickly. It ensures all clients receive the same level of service.

Even though most companies face the same customer success situations, your playbook should reflect your company values, culture, industry expectations, and practices. The playbook provides structure and consistency for the customer success team. You'll likely create different playbooks for various moments of truth along the customer journey or for specific triggers. For example, your playbook could address low product adoption or low usage, or upselling. Then, when a moment of truth happens that triggers the need to upsell, anyone on the team can grab the playbook and have everything they need to upsell the customer.

Developing a playbook will help you accomplish many of your customer-related goals.

Example Triggers for Customer Playbooks

Lifecycle Stage Triggers	Customer Event Triggers	Scheduled Event Triggers	CSM Defined Triggers	Vendor Driven Triggers
ONBOARDING • Send out welcome email • Conduct onboarding workshop • Build out a jointly owned customer success plan **ADOPTION** • Invitation to webinar "3 Quick Ways of Getting the Most of Your Product" • Re-onboarding inactive users **RENEWAL** • Create the ROI deck for monthly check-in call • Make sure all outstanding support tickets are resolved	**A DROP IN USAGE** • Day 1, send the "hey we miss you" emails • Day 4, send a customized email from CSM • Day 9, CSM calls to reach out **CHANGE OF SPONSOR** • Reach out to new hire to set up a meeting to discuss the previous relationship, your insights about their business, and how you can help going forward **LOW NPS SCORE** • Reach out, ask questions, listen! • Follow up and follow through	**QBRs** • Follow QBR guidelines • Happens every quarter **MONTHLY CHECK-IN** • Check in with admin user once every month • See if you can help out or if they need anything **EBR** • Check in with customer executives **RENEWALS** • 180 days out, update risk status of account • 90 days out, send renewal, CSM meets with customer	**UP-TELL DRIVE** • Drive up-tell of certain products • Initiate a marketing campaign or strategy you have in place **CROSS-SELL** • Deliver new Use Cases **CUSTOMER WEBINARS** • Invite Clients to a webinar with an industry influencer • See if you can help out or if they need anything	**RELEASE READINESS** • Speak to clients about the latest release and how it helps them get more value • Value identification around new features **ANNUAL HACKATHON** • Bring in existing users with new users to try new solutions with the software **CUSTOMER CONFERENCE** • Registration email template • Event value discussion • Getting customers to share their experiences and outcomes

www.cspillars.com

Your playbook also needs to be adaptable. The industry is constantly changing and morphing, and your playbook needs to change with it. Your customer is going through an ever-changing environment as well, so you have to update your processes and improve your content to meet their needs.

A playbook is not the same as your standard operating procedures (SOPs). SOPs need to be followed step by step and have to be executed. It's a process. Playbooks are a collection of best practices, examples, successes, and templates that are tailored to specific use cases.

A playbook isn't a step-by-step, word-for-word guide—it's a framework that allows employees to own their roles within the context of the organization. That's what I love most about them. You can build playbooks your own way. You can add a personal element to the playbook, such as your understanding of the customer, the maturity of your customer, your customer's personality, their politics, whatever.

A playbook keeps knowledge in one place for the CSM to access when they need to make a judgment call. Playbooks aren't always perfect, and you can make any adjustments when you discover a strategy that works well—or doesn't work at all.

A SIMPLE TEMPLATE

If you're building your first playbook, start with a simple template, something anyone can contribute to or pick up and use. Also, begin with the fundamentals of a basic task or trigger—you can easily add ideas later and flesh out the details along the way. In fact, it's probably fair to say, "a customer success playbook is never done," because with each new customer and product iteration, you add different product capabilities and new services.

Start with the name of the playbook and trigger that caused you to deploy that playbook. For example, if the playbook were named Customer Onboarding, the trigger event would be "customer signed agreement."

Then add the actions that have to take place once the trigger is activated. Include information that answers the following questions:

- Who owns the action?
- Who are the stakeholders?
- What does the call to action (CTA) look like?
- What are the pieces of collateral—such as presentations, white papers, reference guides, videos, podcasts, and so on—that you can leverage?
- Finally, what are the playbook's system requirements? Once you've delivered the playbook, where are you going to store the information? Is it in a CRM? A financial system? A Google Doc?

Your first templates will be simple, but that's really all you need to get started. As you use the playbook more, you'll discover the information that's most useful and what's missing. Remember, it isn't necessary to have a *perfect* playbook, but it *is* necessary that you have one.

Simple Playbook Template

Play	Trigger	Owner
Example Play: • No Usage • Low Usage • Up-tell Candidate • CSQL	Establish triggers for playbook execution based on key metric thresholds, timings, etc.	Team and Role (when deployed, the playbook will have peoples' names for clarity of responsibility)

CTA	Collateral	Data/Systems
Detail the list of CTAs, include what actions to take, when the actions take place, who owns the actions, who the key stake-holders are, etc.	Access to key templates, presentations, whitepapers, webinars, documentation, usage data, early warning system metrics	Location of collateral, system of record access, visibility of telemetry data of the Customer

www.cspillars.com

The reality is that you need to create playbooks for each part of the customer journey. Here are some playbooks I would start with out of the gate:

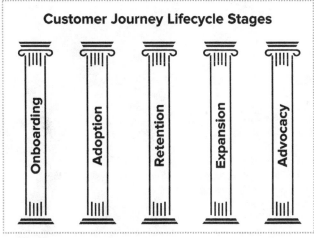

Example Playbooks across the Customer Lifecycle

Customer Journey Lifecycle Stages

Onboarding	Adoption	Retention	Expansion	Advocacy
New Customer Onboarding	Zero Usage	Renewal (xx days out)	Up-tell Opportunities	Secure Reference
First-Time Use	Low Usage	Renewal Risk Identified	Cross-tell Opportunities (Feature Adoption)	Secure Case Study
Customer Success Plan	Drop in Usage	Multi-year Opportunity Identified	Maturity Assessment	Speaking Event
ROI Benchmarking	Low Customer Health	Price Increase Discussion	Value Assessment	Blogs, Social, etc.

Example Playbooks

www.cspillars.com

T3: CUSTOMER HEALTH

Customer health, our third tool, is designed to understand how to be more *pro*active and less *re*active with our customers. We start by understanding our customer's true health.

A lot of companies leave customer health until much later in the development of their customer success organization. When they do decide to focus on it, they do it in an overly simplistic way when they really need to look at all the elements that make a customer healthy (or not).

When I was at Salesforce, the customer health score was called EWS (early warning system). It calculated 127 different inputs for every customer, such as *How many people are logging in every day? Is that number going up or down? How many custom objects are being created? How many reports are being run?*

Over the course of many, many years, Salesforce built the most sophisticated customer health score I've ever seen. As mentioned, EWS could predict customer churn nine months out with 95% accuracy. If churn was predicted, EWS would then deploy the appropriate playbooks to help the CSM save the customer relationship. Salesforce created a finely tuned customer health machine.

Another company, a well-known identity management company, has a much simpler approach to customer health. They discovered that if a customer uses three specific features of their product, they almost never leave. Instead of pulling crazy amounts of data, they only have to ask, "Is the customer using these three features or not?" If the three features *aren't* being used, they know they need to double their efforts around use cases and best practices to show their customer why those specific features will provide them with immense value. This company uses a very different method than Salesforce to determine customer health (and it requires a sophisticated understanding of your product and what differentiates it and its features from competitors in the market), but it works all the same.

No matter which approach you choose, both require years of data collection and cohort analysis (analysis looking at specific groups of customers, over time, and observing how they behave)—to calculate customer health, you're going to have to either partner with or invest in a data analytics platform, data scientists, and data analysts for your customer success team. And the sooner you start, the sooner you'll make better decisions and produce better outcomes for your company. I can't overemphasize the importance of having data-savvy people, either on your team or inside your organization, to help drive your customer health score.

SIX SIMPLE CATEGORIES OF MEASUREMENT

Some of you may be thinking:

But I don't have years to build a data science team and wait for them to tabulate results.

If that's you, don't worry. I'm going to give you six simple categories to measure customer health. I still recommend investing in data analytics for the long run, but gathering the data for the following metrics won't take long and will give you something to work with in the short term.

Before we get started, it's good to note that the metrics below should be measured with each customer's unique goals and objectives in mind. You're measuring the health of each specific customer. That means you need to know what they are *each* looking to achieve by using your product. Generalized metrics (or metrics based on incorrect information) won't be very helpful.

1. **Product Usage:** How often is your customer using your product? What is their license utilization? Is their usage increasing or decreasing? Are there fewer daily active users or more? Are they utilizing the key features of the product that make it sticky? Review what's important to the customer and create metrics for the product.
2. **Business Outcomes:** Customers buy your software because they believe it will deliver their desired outcome. Based on in-depth conversations you've had with the customer, you should know what this outcome is, right? So to create a metric for measuring business outcomes, you need to ask yourself: Are we doing that? Are we making our way down that path? Are we showing evidence? These might be metrics manually entered by the CSM or determined by a business value consulting team.

3. **Customer Sentiment:** There are many different ways to measure customer feedback. There are NPS surveys and CSAT scores. There is also CES, customer effort score. Different teams get feedback from the customer daily, so if you can learn how to funnel it all in, you can add sentiment into your health score.

4. **Relationship Strength:** Have we identified an executive sponsor? Do we have ambassadors/champions/power users identified? How many references have they provided? What rate of surveys are completed? Have they contributed to online blogs or spoken at your company's annual conferences about their awesome experience working with you? We need to know this to gauge account relationship strength.

5. **Services Optimization:** Is the customer utilizing all the service offerings you have that can help them be successful? You may have a tailored professional or partner services, training, or success offerings that will elevate the impact of your software. Is your customer subscribed to these services? And if they are, are they leveraging all the features? If they are, chances are they're getting the best of the best you have to offer. They're getting more value because they're investing in a new service rather than missing out on an opportunity. Bonus: Utilizing those services and features should have a positive impact on customer health.

6. **Support and Operations:** Are your customers using your support team? If they are, what was their experience? How quickly did you answer their phone calls or chat requests? How fast did you resolve their problems? What percentage of interactions were resolved on the first call? How many unresolved tickets are outstanding? What about the SLA you have with your customers? Are you achieving them as promised? What about product quality? Are there bugs and/or feature requests? How good is your documentation? Is your invoicing accurate? You want to understand if the overall experience is a positive one.

At minimum, there are six categories you should pay attention to when calculating your customer health score. In most cases, you can easily work with IT to find these pieces of data in the cloud. Once you do, you can then create your first set of customer health scores.

BE MORE PROACTIVE

When I first got to Looker, customer health scores were predominantly driven by license consumption and the number of logins. It was pretty basic and, as it turns out, not very accurate when it comes to retention probability. We had customers who were "90% healthy" and still leaving, which made no sense.

So we looked into it and, for example, found one churned customer who had 100% license utilization. That drove their health score through the roof. But when the customer churned, we learned it was our company advocate within the organization who left. And when they did, no one else knew how to use our product. The customer had a bunch of people trying to log on to the Looker platform and learn how to derive value from it but ultimately couldn't. One day, we were at 100% utilization, and the next, we received a note saying, "We can't figure out how to use your platform, so we're canceling our subscription."

Measuring customer health doesn't guarantee you success, but it *does* help you become more proactive. Traditionally, in that first wave of customer success, CSMs were trained to be reactive. When there was an issue, they responded like firefighters—as soon as the alarm was raised, they were there in minutes to solve the problem.

But the best CSMs—those who are in the second wave and cresting to the third wave—are those who rise above these incidents, events, and transactions and look at the whole customer journey. Planning ahead and looking at how to remove obstacles in advance—and being what we call "proactive" in the relationship—is what it takes to lead.

Keep in mind, a customer health score shouldn't be equal across the entire customer life cycle because a metric like usage, for example, varies. During onboarding, very few people are using the product, whereas during adoption, you're aiming for operational dependence. If the first question—Is your customer using the product?—carries the same amount of statistical weight (or importance, to put it more plainly) for both onboarding as for adoption, you're going to see some funky numbers. Customer health should consider your customer's place along the customer journey.

Health scores are also a great way to trigger playbooks. If a score is low and when you research the score, you find something you need to address more broadly, put it in a playbook. For example, if we see low feature utilization for a specific product, we can create a playbook that has recommended training, a relevant webinar (or two or three or four), community and blog links, and use cases.

FEATURED FEATURE

One of my favorite types of playbook is a Featured Feature, where the CSM (or product manager) presents (live or recorded) a three-minute demonstration of a key product feature. Over time, dozens of these can be built and used by the customer success, customer marketing, services, or support teams to get adoption of key features.

Health scores are great indicators for the renewals team. If the score is low, it's likely the renewal won't happen, which allows for more accurate forecasting (which helps risk mitigation in business/financial planning) or triggers a playbook to get the customer back on track.

Customer health enables you to have insight into the trajectory of your customer. It allows you to be proactive and think about things to do if you need to reverse negative momentum and get the customer relationship back on track.

T4: CUSTOMER RISK FRAMEWORK

A risk management framework is simply a way of proactively identifying, tracking, and managing risk throughout the customer journey life cycle. Afterall, the customer journey is going to be fraught with dangers along the way. So the goals of the framework are to:

- Better codify "risk"
- Quantitatively identify and measure who are your riskiest customers
- Provide enough lead time to the field and executive team to positively impact the risk
- Feed a red account customer program

So, for me, the customer risk framework consists of eight key risks customers face along with the churn journey map.

CUSTOMER RISK FRAMEWORK

1. **Readiness risk.** This is all about the readiness of the customer to plan, deploy, and gain value from your product. Do they have clear business value and success outcomes defined? Do they have the right services and training defined? Are the supporting pieces of technology in place? Is there a compelling event for launch? These all need to be identified and confirmed to mitigate readiness risk.

2. **Relationship risk** is about losing a key champion, advocate, or sponsor. Who are your key champions, advocates, and sponsors? Is there a chance they may leave? If a key stakeholder resigns and their replacement loves your competitor, suddenly there's a huge risk of losing that business.

3. **Adoption risk** happens when the customer's employees don't use your software or service. The customer signed on the dotted line and completed the implementation process, but if none of their employees are actually using your solution, how long do you think the company is going to pay you for it?

4. **Launch risk** means the deployment of the software is having trouble. Perhaps the customer doesn't have all the supporting pieces of the project in place before you engage. Perhaps your services team or implementation partner are unable to start the custom implementation within a reasonable time frame. Or maybe the approval process is taking much longer than expected. Whatever the issue, if launch risk goes on for too long, the customer is likely to bail on the deal completely.

5. **Fit risk** has to do with using the product the way it was intended. Sometimes your customers will find creative ways to use your software, and when you upgrade it and their creation breaks, they blame you. What happens when they do? They tell you your solution isn't working anymore, and they stop using it completely. Or what if there is a misunderstanding in the sales

process regarding what the actual product is capable of achieving? This, again, is fit risk.

6. **Product experience risk** refers to bugs in the software—that is, "When I click here, the whole thing crashes." It's frustrating for the customer, means lost productivity for the internal teams, and potentially has a huge impact on business. If a customer continuously experiences bugs in the software, they'll get frustrated over time and eventually leave. Or something as simple as a confusing user interface (UI) can lead to a poor user experience.

7. **Feature idea risk** exists when you ignore customer requests, such as, "Could you just change this one thing?" If these requests begin to add up over time, the customer is going to get frustrated. Every time they think about it, they're going to be reminded that you're not listening to them. You're creating a persistent risk. And the impact? Death by a thousand cuts. Eventually, the customer gets so frustrated that they look for another solution that will accommodate their needs, and suddenly, they're out.

Side note: In 2015, I remember reading a blog from a software company called Aha! that referred to feature requests as feature ideas.[1] I'm not saying they invented the phrase, but it always stuck with me as a subtle yet important nuance. When you call it a request, customers get upset when it (usually) doesn't ever deliver. However, if you reframe it as a feature idea, then it's just that, an idea.

8. **Noncontrollable risks** are those you have little to no control over (such as a global pandemic). Macro economically, let's say your customer has been acquired and the new owner no longer wants to use your service. Or you're in the banking industry and new restrictions have made it very difficult for your product to work properly. These are noncontrollable risks, but they are abso-

---

1   "There Are Always More Ideas for Product Managers," Aha!, August 4, 2015, https://www.aha.io/blog/product-managers-there-are-always-more-ideas.

lutely influential. The key to noncontrollable risks is that you can control how you respond. For example, during a pandemic such as COVID-19, having preapproved terms (pausing payments, approved discounts, etc.) for helping customers weather the storm allows the CSM/renewals team to immediately act when a customer experiences hardship (like many did). Customers remember the vendors that helped them versus those that held rigidly to the contract (impacting future purchasing decisions) or took weeks to respond (showing bureaucracy or lack of customer empathy in making decisions).

A customer risk framework helps you identify the persistent risks that are weighing you down over time and prepare for the acute risks that hit you right out of the gate. The customer risk framework identifies the potential risks to your partnership with your customer, and the churn journey map (discussed earlier) identifies where these risks are likely to take place. Playbooks can then be deployed around these risk areas and allow you to know how (and when) to respond in an efficient, repeatable way at scale.

Risk Categories

Category	Descriptions	Indicators	Key Metric(s), e.g.
Sentiment	Poor sentiment of product, engagement or brand	• Poor sentiment of the product or service • Degraded CSAT or NPS scores • Acknowledged frustration from champions or end users • Deteriorating customer relationship	CSAT, NPS, CES
Relationship	Loss of key champions / sponsors	• Loss of key champions / sponsors • No champion or stakeholder • No or insufficient technical resources to support	Stakeholder Identified, Contact Roles, # of Contacts
Adoption	Low adoption	• Low adoption of licenses and/or product features • Low adoption prior to renewal • Low adoption after launch	License Utilization, Consumption, Training & Certification
Launch	Delayed value attainment	• "Stalled" Services Project • Red / Yellow Risk Assessment • Delayed launch or no launch of customer use-case • No/Delayed Value 1	Days to project close, stalled Implementation, TTV

Risk Categories (Cont'd)

Category	Descriptions	Indicators	Key Metric(s), e.g.
Fit	A non-standard use case, or not ready for your solution	• Prerequisite environment for implementation not ready • No long-term strategy or stakeholder in place • Solution fit is appropriate for the challenge to be solved	Risk Assessment
Bugs	Critical bugs impacting customer value attainment	• Prevents the system from providing the value paid for • Atypical use case that doesn't fit into the core competency	Bug Count, Bug Type (P0, P1, P2)
Feature Ideas	Customer Feature Ideas impacting value attainment	• Single critical bug deteriorating customer relationship • Multiple bugs impacting partnership • Single or multiple bugs preventing successful launch	Feature Ideas Count, Open Feature, Ideas time
Non-Controllable	Risk of regulatory or environmental impact to customer (Acquisition, bankruptcy, pandemic, etc.)	• Regulatory policy preventing value from being leveraged in the product • Acquisition • Bankruptcy, layoffs, business viability, pandemic, company turmoil	Industry News, Annual Reports, Government Policy, Pandemics

www.cspillars.com

Special thanks to Brian LaFaille for this table that helps to summarize risk categories a consumable way.

T5: CUSTOMER SUCCESS PLANS

Every new venture needs a plan. When Jeff Bezos and Elon Musk build rocket ships, do you think they just tell their rocket scientists to throw a bunch of metal together haphazardly? No! They follow blueprints! They have a plan!

So why should your customer be any different?

In a nutshell, a Customer Success Plan is a clear statement of how you will deliver value at every stage of the customer's journey with you. A customer journey map identifies the moments of truth between you and your customer, and a playbook tells you how (and when) to respond in a repeatable way at scale. A Customer Success Plan is different—it provides an agreed-upon set of business and technical success criteria to provide value (and find success, along with accountability and efficiency) at every stage. A Customer Success Plan provides consistency throughout the customer's journey, so the focus on meeting (or beating) the customer's expectations remains the same. The two documents run in parallel but provide different value to your customer success organization. One is a strategic overview, and the other is a personalized how-to guide for getting your customer to achieve their desired outcomes.

When should a Customer Success Plan success plan be developed?

As soon as sales hands the client to the CSM (or even sooner). The sooner you create a Customer Success Plan, the sooner you can drive to value for the customer because each plan (if done correctly) should detail exactly what is needed to achieve success. Customer Success Plans should be agreed upon when the project kicks off. Ideally, sales has already captured enough content to ensure key insights will be gained before the start of any Customer Success Plan discussion with the customer. Bonus points: Be seen as so valuable to success that you are part of the presales conversation. Rather than relying on 100% of information being handed over from sales, be part of the discussion and know what's been discussed before the deal is closed. This is really pillar #1.5, which we'll talk about at the end of the book.

SEVEN KEY ELEMENTS

Wondering how to create a top-notch Customer Success Plan? Look no further. Below are the seven key elements that should be included in every high-quality Customer Success Plan.

1. JOINT OWNERSHIP

Most significantly, a Customer Success Plan should be mutually created (and agreed upon) by the customer and the CSM. This isn't like a sales or account management plan that's built internally with the sole purpose of attacking the account to maximize wallet share.

Whereas a sales plan is viewed internally, a Customer Success Plan is something both parties can see. Mutual ownership gets both parties on the same page, so the customer's objectives are clear, both to the customer and the CSM.

2. TRANSPARENCY

True transparency means the agreed-upon Customer Success Plan is visible to the CSM, their customer, and also all relevant parties within your organization.

Everyone who cares about that specific customer should have access to this document. It's as easy as attaching it to your CRM or upload it to a share drive. This way, your sales team can see it, your renewals team can see it, and even your marketing team can see it.

Sharing the document allows those relevant parties to revalidate the plan and make crucial, sometimes customer-saving, decisions in real time. For example, if a customer has pivoted their desired outcome and is now concentrating on a different area of product development than was originally agreed, everyone from sales to customer marketing can adjust their strategies in the account.

When the Customer Success Plan is transparent to all relevant parties within your organization, continuous conversations about the customer and their objectives happen naturally. In addition, increased value is provided.

3. MEASURABLE GOALS

My favorite CEO I used to work directly for (Thomas E. Hogan) would always say, "If I bumped into success in the parking lot, what would it look like?"

A Customer Success Plan must have measurable goals (as well as metrics for achieving those goals) so there's no ambiguity when we achieve them.

Without measurable goals, how will we know when we have achieved the customer's business objectives? How will we know we have provided them with value?

And even more significantly, how will the customer know?

That's where KPIs (key performance indicators) are useful. KPIs are metrics we use, in tandem with the customer, to track our progress toward achieving measurable goals and business outcomes.

Let's say the goal of the Customer Success Plan is to build an elephant. We need a trunk, legs, ears, a tail, and so on. If the goal is to build an elephant, our KPIs would be the individual parts that make up the elephant.

Some people interchange KPIs with business value, but I don't see them as the same. KPIs tell the customer they're getting the value they want along the journey, based on their desired outcome (business value).

Measurable goals with KPIs give us an opportunity to identify and celebrate wins with the customer throughout the customer's life cycle. Celebrating wins is as important as resolving issues throughout the journey.

4. BUSINESS OUTCOME AND VALUE

This key element is simple. The business outcome is the sum of the business objectives the customer is trying to achieve.

When the customer achieves their business outcome, what is the business value? This is a key piece of every Customer Success Plan. We have to capture the business value through financial results or the metrics we use to measure those outcomes.

Once we know what that desired business outcome is, we can then figure out how to deliver value. Maybe the customer's desired business outcome is to add more users and increase revenue. Or maybe they want to create a better experience for their end users to generate increased brand loyalty. Whatever the goal, in order to determine how to accomplish it, we first need to understand what it is so we know how to add value.

We then need to capture that value. For example, if the desired outcome is to add users and increase revenue, find out exactly what those target numbers are. How many users does the customer want to add? What are their revenue goals?

Business value is commonly tied to the financials (revenue and margin). We want to show we're either growing our revenues faster than costs, or we're driving efficiency, because both drive profitability and increase the business value the customer is seeing when they use your product.

5. SKILLS AND CAPABILITIES

What are the skills and capabilities needed from the customer to make sure they can achieve the desired outcome? What do they need to be set up for success?

If the customer is looking to drive more revenue based on data analysis, for example, then we need to understand how to get analytical skills into the minds of the customer to conduct that analysis. We could easily give them the tool that provides them with the business intelligence they're looking for, but if their employees don't know how to interpret the data, ask the right questions, or leverage the information, they're not going to get the right answer. So we could deploy a data culture program or teach data literacy to the customer in order to give them the skills to take advantage of the solution we are offering. Remember, the solution on its own delivers zero value—it's the ability for people to leverage the solution that creates value.

A CSM has the ability to scour their internal organization and figure out who on the team can help achieve the customer's desired outcome.

The skills, capabilities, and people needed to achieve the customer's desired outcome should be included in every Customer Success Plan. And typically, your company (or partners) can provide some of those skills (through customer success, education, or professional services).

6. DYNAMIC

Your Customer Success Plan also needs to be dynamic. It must be easy to update because business (in general) is dynamic, so our Customer Success Plans need to be dynamic along with it.

If your plan or the situation changes, don't be afraid to change and adapt the Customer Success Plan throughout the course of the customer journey. Think about how many of your New Year's resolutions have actually materialized by the end of the year. Life changes things, and likely few (if any) of those resolutions are achieved. You end up achieving other things but not necessarily anything you had set out to achieve on January 1.

Don't be afraid to modify your Customer Success Plan. Look at it as an opportunity to add greater value to your customer's business. It's an action in the right direction and adds to the greater likelihood of success.

So go on. Tweak the plan to align with the customer's goals. Because the last thing you want to do is take off in a gallop in one direction, while the customer is preparing to march in another direction.

7. TECHNOLOGY

Finally, how do we, as a vendor, use technology to help support the customer throughout their journey? What are we bringing to the table that can help facilitate reaching the customer's desired outcome?

List the technology used to support the customer in the Customer Success Plan so it's all in one place and can be easily referenced.

It really is that simple.

Building Customer Success Plans can be intimidating, but it doesn't have to be. Just follow the steps and include the seven key elements listed above. If you do, you'll quickly see it's not as hard as it seems to be.

THE BENEFITS OF CUSTOMER SUCCESS PLANS

There are many benefits to a Customer Success Plan, and every customer should have one.

CREATE TEMPLATES FOR YOUR TEAM

When you, as the customer success leader, create Customer Success Plan templates for your team, not only do you save them time and effort needed to create templates themselves, but you also set expectations for how the team communicates and reports on the customer. It also helps to align your whole company to what's important to that customer. The Customer Success Plan captures the metrics necessary to track success, making it an excellent quality-control tool as well.

CSM TAKES RESPONSIBILITY

There are some cultural benefits, too, that come from building a plan. You're making sure the CSM takes responsibility of the customer and their portfolio. It may sound weird, but simply having a Customer Success Plan creates a feeling of ownership to the CSM assigned to that customer, allowing them to say, "This is my plan for my customer." As this idea builds, the more customers the CSM has.

NO MORE FIREFIGHTING

Customer Success Plans naturally encourage second-wave "big picture" thinking rather than the first-wave firefighting mode of problems, issues, and escalations. When you have a plan that talks about the future and the customer's business outcomes—KPIs and other metrics, whatever they are—it forces the CSM to take a step back and reevaluate.

When things are on fire, most of us sprint to put out the fire. That's just what we do in customer success. But in doing so, we rarely have time to stop and think about what's causing it. A Customer Success Plan developed early on in the relationship with the customer allows us to focus on preventing those fires from starting.

CELEBRATE WINS

If we don't understand the customer's goals or challenges or know how we're going to measure success, what chance do we have of delivering the customer's desired outcome?

Customer Success Plans seen by both the customer and the internal team allow you to share the customer's progress and celebrate small wins, which leads to powerful collaboration. You're giving intelligence to the other teams—such as the renewal team or the accounts team—giving them intel of the customer they wouldn't normally see, which is valuable in discussions and collaboration.

In turn, the customer is reminded of the value you bring and is more inclined to be open to upsell opportunities or to advocate for you to their peers. It's win-win.

BUILD YOUR CUSTOMER SUCCESS PLANS, ONE PILLAR AT A TIME

Customer Success Plana should be used across five of the pillars (the customer journey pillars)—onboarding, adoption, retention, expansion, and advocacy—and teaching you how to build one out of context wouldn't be very helpful. So when we get to the chapter on onboarding (Chapter 4), we'll talk about building Customer Success Plans for onboarding. When we get to adoption (Chapter 5), we'll talk about building Customer Success Plans for adoption.

By the end of the book, you'll not only be aware of the tools, but you'll also see how they apply in every stage of the customer's life cycle.

EXAMPLE CUSTOMER SUCCESS PLAN TEMPLATE

Success Plan: Start Simple

Customer Success Plan *Customer Journey Stage* _____	Account Name:	Presented By:

Company Highlights	Value 1
	Future Objectives

Key Challenges	Key Benefits	Milestones, Actions & Dates	Success Criteria	Success Metrics

www.cspillars.com

Template inspired by SuccessCOACHING, https://successcoaching.co/blog/2019/1/19/single-page-success-plan.

T6: SEGMENTATION

Many of the people I talk to have a different understanding of segmentation, but simply put, more people think segmentation divides your customer base into groups of customers with similar needs so you know how to allocate your resources effectively and efficiently. How you segment is based on what's important and what could change, so don't use past segmentation examples for future needs.

Also, keep in mind you will always have finite resources to manage an ever-growing list of needs, so this is a critical tool.

You can segment to learn which products and services are best suited for each individual group, too. This allows you to maximize your retention and expansion opportunities.

Take a look at this simple segmentation example.

Traditional One-Size-Fits-All Segmentation Model

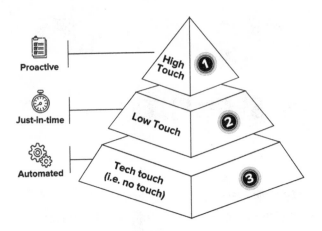

1 Relationship management
- VIP services (e.g. team training)
- Paid-for services (e.g. implementation)
- Escalations (e.g. bugs)
- Opportunities (e.g. expansions and renewals)

2 Focus on outcome > relationship
- One-off services (e.g. reply to email campaign)
- Identify customer at risk (e.g. unsubscribed)
- Identify opportunity (e.g. expansion)

3 Fully scalable
- Help Center
- Automated emails / in-apps
- Video tutorials
- Pre-recorded webinars

www.cspillars.com

Segmentation Model Based on Openview Partners

The triangle at the top represents a small number of essential customers—our high-touch VIPs. These are the customers whom we determine will receive the most support. You have a large number of customers at the bottom who are either new or small in regard to their wallet spend or don't need as many resources anymore to be successful. Those are the customers who receive mostly automated management. And finally, you have customers in the middle, who receive a little bit of both.

When you segment, you're trying to figure out how your most highly skilled resources will have the biggest impact. You're trying to figure out how you can best apply them to meet both the desired outcome of the customer and your company's internal metrics. Considering this is a main function of customer success, segmentation is a CSM's best friend.

HOW DO YOU SEGMENT?

Most companies segment their customer base. If you're reading this book right now, your company has probably segmented theirs.

Let's imagine that you currently have a fantastic customer who pays you millions of dollars each year. They're terrific advocates, they have an incredible center of excellence, and they do their own enablement training. They push you on features and capabilities all the time, so do you need your best CSM on that account all day, every day?

Based on the triangle, yes. They're a top customer. They're high touch. They need someone who is there all day, every day.

But the answer is, "Not so fast."

If you have a customer who is low value and low in risk, you need to focus your effort on retaining that account in an automated way. If you have an account that is extremely high value but low risk, you should put your effort into expanding that account.

Your large accounts don't necessarily need a lot of help. I'm not saying we ignore them or don't spend time with them; I'm just saying their size doesn't automatically guarantee the use of your best resources. It doesn't mean you need to give them 100% of a CSM's time in order to be successful.

If we segment the way sales or marketing segments, we could miss these nuances. Initially, sales and marketing are looking for an immediate transaction that begins the relationship. Success needs its own segmentation best practices because they *continually* manage the current customer environment so they know how to dictate the appropriate investment in resources at any given time. You need to look at the maturity of the customer—where are they in their life cycle or customer journey—and their industry. There are a hundred different inputs you need to consider when you segment (which we'll continue to discuss throughout the rest of this book).

And another example of customer segmentation:

Modern Segmentation Example

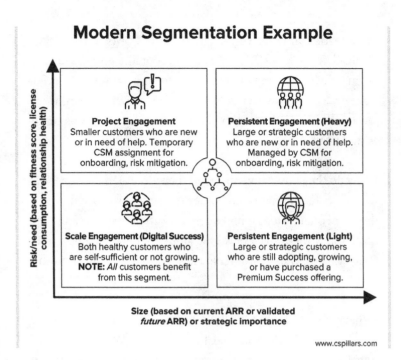

Project Engagement
Smaller customers who are new or in need of help. Temporary CSM assignment for onboarding, risk mitigation.

Persistent Engagement (Heavy)
Large or strategic customers who are new or in need of help. Managed by CSM for onboarding, risk mitigation.

Scale Engagement (Digital Success)
Both healthy customers who are self-sufficient or not growing. **NOTE:** *All* customers benefit from this segment.

Persistent Engagement (Light)
Large or strategic customers who are still adopting, growing, or have purchased a Premium Success offering.

Risk/need (based on fitness score, license consumption, relationship health)

Size (based on current ARR or validated *future* ARR) or strategic importance

www.cspillars.com

SEGMENTING THE SEGMENTATION OF SEGMENTS

The reality is that segmentation can be done in many different ways and should be. For example, you can segment by customer (like we just covered), segment by customer journey phase (as in onboarding), segment on risk/opportunity type such as high-growth potential or at risk, segment the team based on product expertise, and many, many more. Your maturity or market will determine which segmentation should be done and when, but let's look at one we should all do—segment your CSM's time.

SEGMENT YOUR CUSTOMER SUCCESS MANAGERS' TIME

In customer success, segmentation shouldn't only apply to your customer base; it should apply to your customer success team, too.

As a leader, how do you segment your CSMs' time? CSMs typically have a portfolio of customers at any given time. I've seen CSMs with anywhere from 1 to 50 accounts. On a few rare occasions, I've even seen some CSMs own as many as 250 accounts (the CRM tool the customers were using was pretty simple, but still).

How do they know how to spend their time? Do they check in on a low-maintenance customer once a quarter, or should it be more often? Does it make sense for them to read (and then potentially forward) a new case study that may be relevant to only a handful of customers? How do they sort through this matrix?

When you think about it, all day long we segment our time. We look at our calendars and sort our inboxes. We decide which meetings to take and which emails to respond to. We are constantly segmenting, and for CSMs, it permeates everything they do.

When most leaders think about segmentation and success, they immediately think about customers, but we need to think about segmenting the attention of our customer success team, too.

T7: CUSTOMER DELIGHT

One of my favorite movies is *Miracle on 34th Street* (the original, not any of the dozen or so remakes). A scene I particularly like is where Kris Kringle directs one shopper to another store because the desired item is not available at the store they were in. Initially confused but clearly impressed with the honest and useful information, she informs the store manager that she will become a loyal customer (for life).

It seems like a strange choice from a sales perspective, but the long-term effect of such an act is quite remarkable. Santa solved the customer's problem—he told her exactly where to find the toy she needed for Christmas. In return, the store now has a customer for life. Sure, she'll purchase the toy from the other department store, but she'll want to reward the store for solving her challenge by buying everything else from Santa's department store when possible.

Why?

Because Santa delivered value to her. He gave her guidance that was in her best interests, not the interests of the department store.

MORE THAN A HOLIDAY CARD

That scene is a perfect example of customer delight. This tool is tricky because many people believe this concept solely revolves around doing something nice for the customer, such as sending them a gift for the holidays or giving them floor seats to a Lakers game. The reality, though, is this element of customer delight has very little impact on loyalty or growth. *Harvard Business Review* conducted a now-famous study that found these gestures don't influence customer happiness or the expanded use of your product.[2]

This traditional thinking of customer delight is, in my opinion, just the whipped cream on top of the customer success ice-cream sundae. It's something we need to do because it's good for small moments of happiness (and it looks good on social media), but don't make the mistake of thinking that it's going to guarantee your success.

I remember a story from my time at Looker when we were talking to a customer who said, "I've been in the office since six this morning trying to solve this. I didn't even have time for breakfast. I'm just moving as fast as I can." Later that day, one member of the team sent the customer a big box of Frosted Mini Wheats with a note that said, "In case you have another early morning and skip breakfast, this is for you to keep at your desk." The next morning, the customer posted a picture of the cereal box to his social media accounts with the caption that said something like, "I love Looker. These guys are amazing."

It's necessary to give our customers positive experiences, but it's

---

2   Matthew Dixon, Karen Freeman, and Nicholas Toman, "Stop Trying to Delight Your Customers," *Harvard Business Review*, August 2010, https://hbr.org/2010/07/stop-trying-to-delight-your-customers.

likely the direct user isn't the decision maker and has nothing to do with whether the company will decide to renew or expand the use of your product. This individual employee had a great experience, which will immensely help your day-to-day working relationship; it may even boost your NPS score (don't get me started on that yet). However, if that same employee has a bad experience with you in the future, this positive experience will quickly diminish in the user's memory.

For example, if the team at Looker makes a mistake, do you think the customer is going to ignore it because they received a box of cereal? No. But it might reduce the impact of the bad experience, which is a positive.

The way we traditionally think about customer delight is good, and those efforts should be maintained (can you imagine if we just stopped sending holiday cards and thoughtful handwritten notes?), but what if there was a more robust way to think about customer delight? Changing your way of thinking has the potential to dramatically impact your customer success organization.

HubSpot nailed it with their definition:

> "Customer delight is the process of exceeding a customer's expectations to create a positive customer experience with your product or brand to improve loyalty."

ELEMENTS OF CUSTOMER DELIGHT

Traditionally, customer delight has been thought of solely as gift giving, but a more robust understanding of customer delight has the power to transform our business. There are nine elements to modern customer delight.

1. DELIVER VALUE

Modern customer delight is first and foremost about delivering value.

You might be thinking, *That's the point of my job.*

And you're right. The customer has a problem and has bought your software to fix it. By fixing the problem, you and your company are providing business value. *That's the best customer delight.*

Many people forget that customer delight really can (and should be) this simple. They think, *We need to send them some marketing swag. How about a pair of socks or a sticker?* But at its core, the purpose of customer delight is to make a customer happy, and successful outcomes make customers happy.

When we think about modern customer delight, delivering value always has to be priority number one.

2. MAKE IT EASY

Doing business with you needs to be easy. That's priority number two. When they're faced with problems and challenges, make it easy to solve them.

You need to make your customers' interactions and experiences with your products easy. Provide them the training and the materials to learn to properly use the product and best utilize its unique features.

Accessing that training content should be easy, too. When I arrived at one of my previous companies, there were five different systems with five different educational assets (training modules, documentation, webinars, community, etc.). Each system required its own unique login, and for the customers, this was a nightmare. It was really hard for them to solve their problem.

So, for a quick win and to make it simpler, we put all five resources on one page so anyone could easily find them all with one click. Then to truly make it easy for the customer, we created a single sign-on (SSO) capability, which made it easy to navigate in and out of the various sites and find the educational materials that suited them. We made it easier, and it delighted them. As an added benefit of SSO, we now could track and understand what content the user was consuming to help them on their success journey. Through data and analytics, we were also able to realize the impact and value of the content we were producing as we could associate content consumption with outcomes and changes in behavior.

The ultimate end state was to consolidate the five sites down, but in order to deliver quick wins and improved experiences, we did it in three separate stages.

3. BE PROACTIVE
Look for things that will increase value for your customer. "If you did this, you would get this benefit" or, "Did you know you have a problem over here that we can help solve?" People don't think of these moments as generating customer delight, but they do.

4. HELP THE CUSTOMER NETWORK, COLLABORATE, AND SUCCEED

If you help your customer succeed, they will be delighted. This one is significant. Help them by bringing them together with other customers in the same industry; help them network. Promote them inside as well as outside their company. The ultimate compliment—help your champion get promoted.

5. BE RESPONSIVE

When a customer has a problem and reaches out, prioritize that above everything else. Be responsive because that's delightful.

Many companies use chatbots and automated responses for customer support, and I strongly recommend thinking about the message this sends. If your software is causing a problem for the user, it's impacting their day and their ability to be successful at work; a canned response of "We got your request for help" and "You're important to us" is only lip service.

At Looker, we took that very personally. Our customer support organization (the Department of Customer Love) uses a network of human intelligence to delight the customer. We built people into our product, so if you're using the platform and you get stuck, you can click a button, and a live, empathetic human is there to help you.

Last year, there were hundreds of thousands of customer interactions; our average response time was 23 seconds, and more than 90% of all callers had their problem resolved on their first call. We've made it easy for people to solve their problems. There is a lot of customer delight here, and it didn't impact the company's gross margin either (a common reason why people choose the automated route) because of the benefits this kind of delight brings from loyalty, retention, expansion, and advocacy.

6. GIVE CONSTRUCTIVE FEEDBACK INSIDE YOUR COMPANY

If you see a problem or an issue a customer faces with other departments, give that department the insight. Remember, you are the voice of the customer inside your organization.

For example, every time someone has an interaction with support, they get a survey. If they interact five times, they get—you guessed it—five surveys. This is probably annoying for the customer, meaning customer success needs to work with whichever department is responsible for sending those surveys, and figure out a way to improve the experience for the customer. Okay, so you set up a rule that says only one survey for every five interactions with support. But now they get a survey from their services implementation, and a CSM sends them a voice of the customer survey. Then they get their support survey. You get the idea.

When the customer's experience isn't great, it's the CSM's job to bring attention to whoever is ultimately responsible for that experience. CSMs are responsible for improving the customer's experience and for giving relevant internal departments constructive feedback on how to do that. CSMs need to rise above the artificial silos companies put in the way of the customer experience.

7. ANALYZE AND ACT ON CUSTOMER FEEDBACK

Your customers are often the best source for learning how to give them more value, if you know how to tap into it. Ask your customers for their opinion, but be prepared to respond to what they're asking you to do (even if it's a no). If you can't, you shouldn't bother to ask at all. Asking for opinions without acting on them often just makes it worse.

Also (and this ties into the element *Be Responsive*), if a customer tells you they have a problem (solicited or unsolicited), you should reach out to them immediately. When you do, the customer will be delighted.

8. BE TRANSPARENT

This really means two things. First, it means being transparent with the customer whenever a change is made, including changes to personnel. In the past, I didn't do a good job of communicating with customers about personnel changes, and it was upsetting. Now I change out CSMs in a more thoughtful, intentional way.

Second, when you make a mistake, you need to be transparent. Be up front and tell your customer. Also, tell them how you're going to remedy the mistake. They're going to find out anyway. But if you tell them sooner rather than later, the more delighted they'll feel in spite of the situation.

My team once helped a customer connect to a database but connected to the wrong one, which caused a security breach. My team fixed the issue quickly, and even though I could have kept the incident a secret, I didn't. I came clean with the customer because it's the right thing to do. I may think I "fixed" the problem, but what if I didn't? There could be something I don't know that could put my customer (or *their* customers) in jeopardy. Being completely transparent is the right thing to do.

You should also be transparent about positive things, such as upcoming feature additions or new products. If your solution is going to be featured in an article or at a conference, let your customers know. This will leave them feeling like a partner who is aiding in your success.

9. SEND A PERSONALIZED GIFT (THE TRADITIONAL THINKING OF CUSTOMER DELIGHT)

Once you have delighted your customer by being proactive and helpful, making it easy and driving value, then and only then can you send your customer a gift. This can be a nice card, a cake, or a meaningful box of cereal.

Your gift needs to be personalized, especially if it's an unused marketing swag thrown together in a box that's shipped out by your office manager.

Let's make it meaningful and personalized. That's delightful.

Customer delight is more than a holiday card and a client appreciation dinner. A robust understanding of customer delight and all its facets has the power to transform your business (and your customers).

T8: VOICE OF THE CUSTOMER

Welcome to a new age. Companies now use their user experiences (rather than their products) to compete for business. Why did this happen? Product technologies were evolving so fast (they still are) that everyone was leapfrogging over everyone else. It looked like this:

"We added this new feature."

"And we added this feature!"

"Well, WE added this feature."

"THIS feature is the greatest feature of them all!"

You get the point.

In the current marketplace, the only way you're going to differentiate yourself is through the experience you give your customers. That's why customer experience is now a necessary business function. In the past, customer experience was considered support. Most people thought, "Oh, the customer experience is the experience they have when they call support," but over the years, the notion of experience has become more compelling and strategic, and rightly so.

As we've discussed, we're in a customer-dominated, subscription-driven environment (where retention of the customer is preeminent). So how do we know the type of customer experience we're delivering? How do we know how the customer feels about the experience we're giving them?

The voice of the customer is all about listening, analyzing, and acting on customer feedback. This tool should be utilized across your entire enterprise to make sure you retain, expand, and create advocates within your customer base.

You may not realize the treasure trove of information you are capturing about the customer along the entire customer journey. It could be through survey responses, escalations, support tickets, email marketing campaigns, or even one-on-one conversations. Throughout the customer journey, information about the customer is delivered to us constantly. The ability to capture that information and put it in a unified place where it can be analyzed is essential to better understand where the customer is along their journey and what their experience has been with your brand.

The Aberdeen Group conducted a study called "The Business Value of Building a Best-in-Class VoC Program" and found that companies investing in customer feedback programs experience *higher* customer retention and employee engagement. These same companies also spend *less* on customer service.[3]

---

3   Steven MacDonald, "Voice of Customer: How to 10x Your Business with VoC Data," SuperOffice. com, last updated January 4, 2021, https://www.superoffice.com/blog/voice-of-customer/.

A QUICK WORD ON SURVEYS

When I got my first car, my grandfather said, "Looks like you're gonna need some insurance."

"I don't think I can afford the insurance," I said.

"Then you can't afford the car."

When it comes to cars and insurance, you can't have one without the other. The same goes for surveys. Don't survey a customer if you're not prepared to immediately respond.

Let me give you a real example I experienced recently. I had a horrible experience at Denver International Airport going through the CLEAR lane. Frustrated, I responded to a survey I received, and the general manager of CLEAR, for that location, addressed my feedback the *same day*. He told me he understood my frustrations, explained to me why my experience had been poor that day, and then explained to me what he was doing to fix the problem and prevent it from happening again. Because he responded immediately, I know he values my opinion, and as a result, I will be a CLEAR customer for life.

IF YOU BUILD IT, THEY WILL COME

Voice of the customer captures actionable feedback and then analyzes it to find commonalities. Take all the information and data you have, and once amassed, look for trends and themes to help you improve. Then work out the challenges and opportunities. You might ask yourself, *How can I improve the relevant areas of the business while focusing on providing value to the customer?*

We've established how substantial a voice of the customer capability is to your customer success organization, so now let's talk about how to build one. Here are six simple steps.

1. SURVEY TIMING

CLEAR sends a survey out to their customers every time the service is used. When it comes to your voice of the customer program, the first thing you need to understand is when to collect the voice of the customer content. Timing is everything. Consider the touch points and behavior on the customer journey that should trigger a survey.

I recommend gathering feedback after onboarding and adoption (pillars 2 and 3, Chapters 4 and 5, respectively) and anytime you introduce a new feature. We're always capturing the voice of the customer through all of our work actively listening and monitoring the community and social channels, but when we manually insert a voice of the customer survey, we can collect customer feedback in real time. We can better understand whether we've hit the mark and if the customer is in a good place. If you see a change in customer usage or behavior or if a project has been fully implemented or a milestone achieved, send a survey.

2. RESPONDING TO FEEDBACK

But when it comes to the voice of the customer surveys, as I said before, if you can't respond to your customer's feedback quickly, you're better off not asking in the first place. This is the second thing you need to understand when creating your voice of the customer program. Nothing is worse than being asked your opinion, and then having that opinion ignored.

When I gave CLEAR my opinion after a disappointing experience, if no one had reached out to me that day, it would have left me feeling even more disgruntled. If you can't respond to your customers' negative feedback on the same day, don't bother. It will only backfire as it shows you're surveying for internal metrics (vanity metrics) and not because you're interested in listening to the customer.

3. SHARE CONTENT

The third thing you need to do is share your voice of the customer content across your entire company. Even though this responsibility is typically owned by customer success, it is truly cross-functional. If people complain about the product or service, we need to share that feedback with those teams. Inversely, if someone has an incredible experience with them, we need to let the team know that, too. Imagine how many surveys are sent out by support or services (or product or marketing) and your CSMs don't have visibility into the responses from their customers.

Our job as customer success professionals is to take the information we receive from our voice of the customer tool and disseminate it and share it with the rest of the company. It is up to us to celebrate wins and strategize how to remove any friction from the customer's world.

4. PERSONALIZED JOURNEYS AT SCALE

There is nothing I hate more than a canned, automated response.

"Thank you for your feedback! You've made a difference! Cheers!"

Today, technology can make things tailored and personalized, simply by using your name, which is why I find canned responses (especially to negative feedback) incredibly annoying. When you get a response back that doesn't use your name, you can immediately tell no one really cares about you in this interaction. You took the effort to give them feedback, and all they could do in return was send an automated, impersonal response? It's clear that they put in zero effort—the bare minimum we'll call it.

If the response comes back with their name, at least they'll say, "Well, they [the system] know who sent them the feedback, that's good, but it's likely still automated." So imagine the possibilities if you personalized the response even further. You'd hit it out of the park.

"Thanks for your feedback, Wayne. We value you as a member and want to thank you for staying loyal to us for the last five years. Looks like you're traveling a lot this year!"

When I get a response like that, I'm impressed. The response is still automated because the information can be pulled from your CRM system (it's not like someone is sitting there researching customer tenure), but it demonstrates you put more effort into your response—you care about the experience. Not only does the customer feel appreciated, but they're also encouraged to continue to provide you with feedback. And who doesn't love getting their Chick-fil-A end-of-year report telling them what they ordered the most that year (chicken nuggets was mine, in case you were wondering). Personalized journeys at scale right there!

5. ESCALATE NEGATIVE FEEDBACK

If you get negative voice of the customer feedback, treat it like a product escalation case. For example: "The product's on fire! It isn't working and it's impacting our business!" So everyone jumps on a call immediately to strategize how to address the problem.

Treat negative voice of the customer feedback as something that needs to be examined and solved right away. "This is a problem and we need to go fix it." Don't just sit there and say, "Oh, it's a shame they're having a bad experience. Let's make sure we respond within 72 hours." Potentially too much damage (to their business and your brand) will take place within that time frame. Treat it like an escalation.

6. TAKE IT FOR WHAT IT IS

Voice of the customer is about learning how to improve the customer's experience. It isn't about trying to make life difficult for you as a vendor or customer-focused leader. This isn't about you; it's about genuine feedback from your customers. So take it as that.

What you decide you act on doesn't necessarily need a big, involved plan. Sometimes all it takes is a quick response. When you respond quickly, you get the customer's attention. If you contact that customer within the first hour of receiving their feedback, you have the opportunity to have a powerful, positive impact.

T9: QBRS AND EBRS

In-person meetings can be a powerful tool. It really allows you to build a solid relationship with your customer that can have a lasting impact at both a business and personal level. Of course, COVID-19 showed us that it's not always possible to have these in-person meetings like we were used to, but it's important to note we can still have impactful meetings with our customers (via tools such as Google Meet, Zoom, Teams, etc.). These meetings are an opportunity to reach your key stakeholders as well as showcase your wins; they are a way to prove you're delivering value. Oftentimes, I have heard people exchange these two types of meetings, but they aren't the same thing.

WHAT IS A QUARTERLY BUSINESS REVIEW?

A quarterly business review (QBR) is pretty straightforward. It's a regular meeting with your customer to discuss project impact (metrics, value one, SLAs, current initiatives, etc.) and how you can continue to support them and help them be successful.

A quarterly meeting works for most customers but not all. Sometimes QBRs can happen more or less frequently, depending on the situation, company maturity, or even the customer's current project list. Whether it's every two months, two times a year, or truly quarterly, the purpose of a QBR is to meet regularly with your customer so you can track their engagement with your product and find out how you can help them achieve success.

Now that you know what a QBR is, let's learn how to best plan for and execute one. I have put together a checklist of eight items every CSM should consider when preparing for the meeting.

1. PLANNING

First, you need to generate interest in the QBR so your stakeholders attend. When you send your customer an email to schedule it, include a data-driven insight you want to discuss.

"Hello, customer! We noticed your adoption spiked 15% this quarter. I'm going to cover that in our next meeting."

Or, "Hello, customer. We recently benchmarked you against your peers and discovered you are 10% below average when it comes to feature adoption. We'll go over it in more detail in our next meeting."

When you include a detail in the email that creates an aha moment, your customer is encouraged to attend the meeting because their interests are piqued. They think, *Ooooh, I want to learn more about that.*

2. AGENDA REVIEW

The QBR is primarily for your customer, so you want to make

sure they have input. As soon as you're done crafting the meeting's agenda, send it to your stakeholders so they're able to review it in advance. Then encourage them to add anything else they'd like to discuss.

"This is our typical agenda, but is there anything else you'd like to cover? What do you need to get out of this meeting?"

3. CURRENT SITUATION

Before the meeting even starts, you first need to determine if there are any changes to the process, product, org structure, goals, or metrics. That means, you need to establish the customer's current situation before you ever get to the meeting.

Ask, "Is this still your goal? Is this still what you're trying to shoot for in regard to our partnership?"

Your customer's goals will change as their business priorities change, and you want to make sure you're on top of it.

4. PREVIOUS QUARTER

Once you've confirmed your customer's business objectives, you want to review the previous quarter's failings and accomplishments. Give your stakeholders a quick summary so everyone is on the same page.

"Let's look at how we did last quarter. We had these issues and achieved these milestones. Here is last quarter's data about adoption, your users, product searches, and licenses."

5. CHALLENGES AHEAD

After you've reviewed the previous quarter, move into a conversation about upcoming challenges you want to address with your customer. This will create an open line of communication with your customer so that you may manage their expectations as you help them solve problems.

For example, during the Coronavirus pandemic of 2020, almost every customer had to rewrite their plans and strategies for the year. This is a great example of why we need to ask in every QBR what future challenges are ahead and how to consistently confirm what those goals and challenges are.

6. UPCOMING PRIORITIES

Ask about their goals and discuss the action plan for the upcoming quarters. The driving question is, *What do we need to achieve before we get together again?* Once we can answer those questions, together with our customer, we can create our list of priorities for the upcoming quarters.

7. UPTELLING SOLUTIONS

This is where you need to keep the Expansion Pillar in mind. When you create your presentation for the QBR, throw in a slide or two about a case study highlighting a new feature or product you believe would help the customer achieve additional success.

"I want to share with you an amazing case study for a feature we launched last month. The company that used it is in the same space as you and they were able to accomplish X, Y, and Z. If it produced this outcome for them, I thought it may be of interest to you."

This is a subtle way to "uptell" the customer about additional solutions (and help them be successful) without sounding "salesy." Remember, our goal is to drive increased value for our customers at all times. This is just another way to do it.

If things are in a good place with the relationship, it's an excellent time to get a commitment for a reference, referral call, case study, peer review, or any number of advocacy assets.

8. MEETING SUMMARY

Conclude the meeting with a summary. Cover any changes to the current situation and the previous quarter's highlights. Review the upcoming challenges as well as priorities, and finally, set a date for the next meeting.

QBRs create an open dialogue with your customers. They keep them informed and let you know whether you're still on track. If the customer is small, you may be able to automate the way you deliver the QBR, but whether it's low touch, medium touch, or high touch, it's the best method to check in with the customer and confirm priorities. Every CSM must be able to deliver one, either virtually or face-to-face.

AND AN EXECUTIVE BUSINESS REVIEW?

An executive business review (EBR) should present information at a much higher level, with a focus on executive leadership. It is one of the most influential meetings you will have with your customer all year, yet it's the one most organizations tend to forget. QBRs happen frequently, across the industry, but EBRs? Not so much.

Less tactical and less operational than a QBR, an EBR is typically reserved for your customer's executive leadership team because it's a high-level review of the value your product is providing the customer. When you draft an EBR, you should be thinking along the lines of, *Who is my stakeholder's boss? How do I co-present to my stakeholder and their boss the value my product has offered and will continue to offer them?*

An EBR is a way to move up the value chain, promote your stakeholder's brand inside their own company, and share wins with the executive leader. It's a strategic meeting that should focus on reinforcing the value in your customer ROI. It should also validate the goals of the organization, because like you did with your QBRs, you're building a partnership through open dialogue. The only difference is now you're doing it at an executive level.

EBRs should be scheduled twice a year. I typically recommend scheduling one at least three months before the customer's renewal because if the meeting goes well, it may help move the renewal along faster. I have seen executives stop pushing on price when they're negotiating terms, and I've even seen some CSMs contact a stakeholder's executive directly to ask for their help.

"We're having trouble with this renewal. Can you step in and assist?"

More often than not, the executive will call whoever they need to call and say, "Just get it done."

Plus, when you reach out and ask for help, you're engaging executive-level advocates, which is always a good thing.

ELEVEN SUGGESTIONS FOR KICK-BUTT EBR PLANNING

Because EBRs are substantially different than QBRs, I've got some hints and tips on how to plan and execute one effectively.

1. **Keep It Short:** Your EBR should be 30 minutes long at the most. These are executives, and getting even an hour of an executive's time is hard. You need to be able to do it in 30 minutes.

2. **Plan Ahead:** When it comes to planning the meeting itself, establish the who, what, where, and when far in advance so the executive has plenty of time to reschedule if needed.

3. **Confirm Meeting Attendees:** If the executives and major decision makers can no longer attend the meeting, reschedule it. Don't travel to your customer's office just because you've already booked a flight and hotel. Reschedule the meeting and then rebook travel.

4. **Make It Interactive:** Throughout the meeting, you want to keep the executives engaged. Ask for positive and negative feedback and keep it interactive.

5. **Focus on ROI:** Remember to focus on business value and ROI. If you can do a value assessment and prove value, do it.

6. **Roadmap:** It's important to expose executives to what's coming on the roadmap and highlight areas known to be impactful on their business's success.

7. **Track Goals:** You should also track goals from previous EBRs. Share them in the current EBR and reiterate what will be shared in the next one. One key addition here is for both you and your customer to present jointly agreed and recommended changes to the Customer Success Plan.

8. **Rely on Data:** Today, more and more executives rely on data to make decisions, so when you plan your EBR, make sure you include data-driven recommendations. Don't give them your opinion or your gut feeling; give them data.

9. **Listen Actively:** Listen carefully to the executives' questions and try to read between the lines. Executives are always thinking four moves ahead and may not ask direct questions but instead allude to something else seemingly unrelated. You have to actively listen to make sure you pick up on their unspoken cues.

10. **Don't Be Defensive:** If the executive brings up challenges (they most surely will if you don't proactively), respond with confidence and respect. Don't get defensive. They hate that. "Thank you for pointing that out. Yes, this is a challenge we've faced, but we've mobilized internally and have a plan to avoid them in the future. You have my commitment that our team will do better, and I will prove that in the next EBR."

11. **Follow Up:** Make sure you follow up and post the meeting. Put together a very detailed action plan, with next steps and needed materials, and put it in a deck. Cover all your bases and make sure you've captured everything. Don't forget a quick summary at the beginning of the email summarizing the more comprehensive details further down in your report.

As businesses and companies change and transform, make sure you work with your customer to reset EBR cadence expectations. For example, if you did an EBR with any travel industry company before the COVID-19 outbreak, you probably should have done another one soon after travel restrictions were put in place. Waiting too long could have seen your software jettisoned before you knew what was happening.

But don't just have an EBR to have an EBR. There needs to be an authentic need. "We know a tough time is coming and we want to help you through it. We have some ideas we'd like to share. Are you interested?"

An EBR focuses on ROI and executive engagements, whereas a QBR is operationally focused. However different, both are needed for an effective customer success organization.

THOUGHT LEADERSHIP SERIES: IRIT EIZIPS

Irit Eizips, Chief Customer Officer and CEO at CSM Practice, is a world-renowned expert on customer success and customer value strategies and methodologies. Since 2013, Irit has been pivotal in shaping customer success best practices. Her company (founded the following year) is the first customer success strategy consulting firm in the world and helps companies accelerate profitable growth through the design and implementation of customer success frameworks. Eizips shares her knowledge on the importance of customer business reviews as an effective tool to provide value and learn more about your customers.

CUSTOMER BUSINESS REVIEWS

The customer business review is one of the most vital activities a CSM must perform to discuss value with their clients. Also known as a quarterly business review (QBR) or an executive business review (EBR), this client-facing session is, at its most basic definition, a group discussion you have with your clients. The focal point of the business review revolves around the outcomes and priorities of your customers. For example, what can be done to accelerate their business growth, and what are their business's most urgent desired outcomes. Following up with tangible recommendations to actualize value based on the desired outcomes identified during a business review is also crucial for a business review process.

BUSINESS REVIEW CADENCE

Based on the terminology itself, customer success practitioners may think a QBR is strictly a once-per-quarter activity. But the cadence for business reviews should be determined based on the customer attributes. The larger and the more significant the customer is to your business, the higher the frequency of the customer reviews and the resources you'll dedicate to this process.

The appropriate frequency of customer business review sessions can be determined based on your customer segmentation, which at its most simplistic form, can be classified into three types: strategic, mid-market, and small.

CUSTOMER SEGMENTATION	CUSTOMER SUCCESS ENGAGEMENT	BUSINESS REVIEW FORMAT	BUSINESS REVIEW CADENCE
Strategic/large	High touch	On-site, if possible	2–3 times a year
Mid-market	Mid-touch	Online	Once a year
Small	Tech/low touch	Digital	As needed

BUSINESS OUTCOMES DISCUSSIONS

As a CSM, you will act as a consultant for your customers in guiding them toward success. Typically, during a business review session, customers are asked to identify their desired business outcomes. A good CSM will then develop a Customer Success Plan to ensure that those business outcomes are delivered as discussed. However, there is a downside to this approach since it assumes that customers know what they want, which is not always the case.

To further understand the context of conducting a successful customer business review, during the customer business review session, you must focus on the list of business outcomes your solution can additionally provide to an organization of their size or in their industry. Don't try to use the same list for a different industry or company size because it will dilute the value of customer business review and your ability to promote a highly meaningful relationship with the client.

To invoke an outcomes discussion with customers, a CSM may also leverage customer benchmark data, survey results, or a maturity scoring model.

PREPARING FOR A CUSTOMER BUSINESS REVIEW THE CUSTOMER SUCCESS WAY

Presenting new ideas that generate new business outcomes for your customers in a customer business review can go a long way to provide value to them. This way, it will increase your customers' perceived value, especially when you prove the value of your new ideas to their business goals.

It is either you avoid lousy customer business review sessions, or your client relationship will sink accordingly. It is up to you, as a CSM, to make a great and meaningful customer business review, to step into the customer business review leadership role, and obtain a more productive customer success management experience.

There are several ways a CSM can identify opportunities to add value to the customer. To further magnify perceived value and propel value discussions with customers during a business review, there are three methods for detecting value opportunities and relevant business outcomes:

- **Observe on-site product process:** Analyze the product usage and closely watch how clients work with their products. What does product usage look like along the trends, which features are being used, and which are not? With this analysis, you can personally observe if they are using the product effectively and which part of the process they fail to execute and need coaching.

- **Identify ways to improve the process:** By observing how they use their products, we can assess and identify how to improve the process and effectively use it. Through the data gathered from the observation stage, customer success teams can develop action plans to improve their product maximization process.
- **Data poll process:** Conduct an automated data poll process showing the areas where they are doing well and the areas that need improvement.

In a nutshell, a customer business review can help you drive a big impact and maximize your clients' value. Always look at the bigger picture to assess the situations and the status of your clients so you can identify what they need to achieve their goals and desired outcome for their business.

T10: METRICS

The last tool in our Customer Success Toolbox is metrics. Like a scorecard, metrics are the measurements you monitor and evaluate, to track progress on goals, like things you would deliver to the board of directors (or shareholders, if you're a public company). When we think about metrics, reporting, and customer success, we need to keep both the customer and the company in mind. That means, we need to measure two different things:

- How are my customers doing?
- How are we doing as a company?

When you think about these two questions, you can start to develop the metrics you need to measure success. You can have 10, 20, 30, or 50 metrics—and if you do, you should write them all down—but from my perspective, you gotta start with these five metrics first.

1. CUSTOMER LOGO CHURN

This is the number of customers that leave. It's as simple as that.

2. GROSS REVENUE RETENTION

This metric measures revenue lost from the existing customer base spend and does *not* include any benefits from expansion revenue (upsell or cross-sell) and price increases. Gross revenue retention (GRR) is different than customer logo churn because you don't have to lose a customer to lose revenue. A customer may renew but only at 50% of historical spend. You still have the logo because the customer didn't churn, but 50% of the revenue churned. GRR measures that churn.

Let me give you a quick example. The highest GRR each customer can have is 100%. Because we ignore any increases in revenue, the most a customer can "renew" is the existing spend they have, also known as 100%. If they spend less (if they revenue churn) and renew at a lower amount, the GRR will come down. So if the customer's GRR is 90%, that means 10% of your revenue churned.

For me, it's a better metric than net retention rate (see below) because it tells you the long-term health of your customer base. When using net retention rate metrics, a huge expansion in a large customer may "hide" the churn revenue of a lot of other customers (or the long-term health of your customer base).

3. NET RETENTION RATE

Net retention rate (NRR) measures what the existing customers spend with us today. This will include increased consumption, price increases, additional licenses, or products they've added. NRR should include all the extra items they buy and, unlike GRR, can be above 100% (and the higher the better).

In other words, is my cohort of customers from one year ago

paying us more now than they were 12 months ago? Is my company growing without having to add net new logos?

NRR is a very important metric. If you're a private company and want an IPO and to go public, you should aim to have a minimum 115% NRR. That means growing at a 15% rate without adding any additional customers. If your NRR isn't above 100%, it means you're doing a horrible job of retaining existing customers, and neither Wall Street nor Main Street will look at that favorably.

The opposite is true, too. I remember when Zoom went public and had an NRR of 140% (and that was before the pandemic). That was mind-blowing to me. Other companies with the highest valuations had great NRRs, such as Workday, Datadog, Twilio, and more. Super impressive!

4. EXPANSION ANNUAL RECURRING REVENUE

Expansion annual recurring revenue (EARR) or expansion ARR is the percentage of new revenue that comes from existing customers. There's no real benchmarking for EARR because all industries are different, but I recommend tracking it because I think it's important for customer success. This metric will tell you how successful you are at *uptelling* your existing customers. It also helps to articulate the value of a great customer success organization as our mission is to not only onboard, get adoption, retain, and create advocates from our customer base but also to partner with sales and product teams to expand value and result in revenue expansion.

5. CUSTOMER EFFORT SCORE

The final metric is customer effort score (CES), and it's controversial because it's not solely owned by customer success. Everyone uses NPS, but CES is a *much* more valuable tool. (Yes, begin the controversy! More on how I really feel about NPS in the Advocacy Pillar in Chapter 8.) Not only does it evaluate the ease in which a customer believes their recent challenge was solved; it can also be used across multiple departments.

For example, if a customer accesses your company's support system, a CES would measure how easy it was for the customer to interact with that system. It would also measure whether the customer's problem was solved and how effortless it was to solve it. A CES is how you know if you're making it easy for your customer.

A subsidiary of Gartner, the Corporate Executive Board Company (CEB) found a correlation between improving a customer's CES and increased customer loyalty. On a 7-point scale, if a customer's CES increased from 1 to 5, their loyalty improved by 22%.[4]

These are the five key metrics every customer success organization should start with, but there are many others to pay attention to as well. There are metrics you may want to report on but not share with the outside world—for example, financially driven metrics such as CLV and customer retention cost (CRC). There's also average revenue per account, customer health score, product usage, engagement, and more. Each of these metrics are essential in their own right and can be used to measure the effectiveness of customer success within your company.

---

4   "Ultimate Guide to Customer Effort Score CES," CustomerThermometer.com, accessed January 19, 2021, https://www.customerthermometer.com/customer-retention-ideas/ultimate-guide-to-customer-effort-score-ces/.

Finally, it's good to remember that although metrics are used to report wins (and failures) to stakeholders (and shareholders), they are also used to make decisions about the overall direction of the business and the customer success function. For example, if a large cohort of customers churn after year one, take a look at your onboarding and adoption programs.

Customer Success Toolbox

T1	**Moments of Truth (MOT)**	• Where great customer success experience begins
T2	**Playbooks**	• A guide to how CS is done at your company, including best practices, protocols, templates, strategies, and more
T3	**Customer Health Score**	• Score + Trend = Appropriate Action • Human-first approach
T4	**Customer Risk Framework**	• A way to identify, classify, and action risk in your account
T5	**Success Plans**	• A blueprint by which both you and your customer can achieve mutual success
T6	**Segmentation**	• A formalized way to break your customers into cohorts allowing different approaches for success • A way to break out time commitments for your CSMs
T7	**Voice of the Customer**	• How we capture the customers' experiences, preferences, and challenges to turn into actions
T8	**QBRs/EBRs**	• QBR: To review the Customer Success Plan and determine progress towards achieving desired outcomes • EBR: Demonstrate to the economic buyer the value they are receiving and future plans
T9	**Customer Delight**	• The process of exceeding a customer's expectations, delivering a positive customer experience with your product or brand to improve loyalty, and delivering their desired outcome
T10	**Metrics**	• To measure and act on the customer experience being delivered by your organization, product, and company

www.cspillars.com

Now that we have the tools nailed down, let's jump into the seven pillars—the framework for your company and your customer's journey with you. We'll use the tools we have at our disposal to operationalize customer success.

PART TWO

THE SEVEN PILLARS

The Seven Customer Success Pillars

Customer Journey Lifecycle Stages

- Operationalize CS
- Onboarding
- Adoption
- Retention
- Expansion
- Advocacy
- Strategic Advisor

www.cspillars.com

CHAPTER 3

PILLAR #1: OPERATIONALIZING CUSTOMER SUCCESS

"VALUE MANAGED"

The Seven Customer Success Pillars

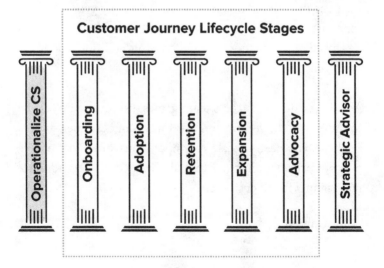

Customer Journey Lifecycle Stages

Operationalize CS · Onboarding · Adoption · Retention · Expansion · Advocacy · Strategic Advisor

www.cspillars.com

The first pillar, Operationalizing Customer Success, is arguably the most important pillar but is the least understood. It is the least understood because it's the least mature. There is an air of mystique surrounding this pillar, which is why it often gets skipped or glossed over. But Operationalizing Customer Success is the pillar that allows all the other pillars to function properly. Without it, the framework is dead in the water. That's why it's critical to understand how the pillar works and how to incorporate it into your current customer success function.

Companies new to customer success often miss this crucial step. They deploy a first-wave version of customer success—the version that was used more than 15 years ago. They hire a couple of people in customer success and say, "Go make the customers happy! Do whatever it takes!" But their customer success isn't operationalized. The CSM doesn't know what to focus on, so they roll up their sleeves and handle every unique challenge and problem that comes up. This works at first because having someone focus on customer success is better than no one. What happens over time, though, is as the company gets more and more successful and adds more and more customers, it becomes less efficient to hire more CSMs. Throwing additional bodies at the problem is very expensive.

As your customer success team grows, however, you'll need to move into the second and third waves of customer success. To do so, you need to scale your operations, hire more people, and put processes in place to make sure your operations are consistent with all customers.

In a word or three, you have to operationalize customer success.

MAXIMIZE YOUR IMPACT

When a customer buys a piece of software, the software itself doesn't do anything other than hold the promise of transformation. The customer believes the software can solve the problem, but the software doesn't actually do anything until you learn to use it and adopt it as part of your everyday workflows.

The overarching goal of customer success is to deliver desired outcomes to our customers, and to do that, you have to first understand all of that software's capabilities. Then you have to create tools, processes, and workflows so that it's easy for the customer to take advantage of the capabilities that will best serve their business. Customer success is valuable because it bridges the gap between the promise made during the sales cycle and the solution the software has promised to provide.

Operationalizing Customer Success is the first pillar in the Seven Pillars of Customer Success because that enables us to maximize the impact of our customer success organization. We need to define what the CSMs should focus on and set them up to deliver a consistent customer experience. We also need to ensure that our capabilities are scalable as we grow. Finally, we need to provide common vernacular—words and language—that everyone will use so there's no confusion. Operationalizing customer success is about providing the tools, processes, and workflows to ensure all of those things happen.

There are a lot of different definitions and interpretations of operationalizing customer success because the function has yet to be standardized. People struggle to understand customer success in general, and there's a difference of opinion on the definition of operationalize customer success. So I've created my own definition:

> *The customer success team delivers proven best practices at scale, in a repeatable way and with efficiency, to drive the desired outcome of your customer and your company, wrapped in an exceptional customer experience.*

We are trying to apply a systematic approach to automating tasks and orchestrating specific operational processes. Once we do, we then define and measure goals that align with the business priorities of both the customer and our company, delivering value.

We want to *deliver proven best practices* because as we learn as an organization (and capture that knowledge and share it with others), we can grow and scale. We get *repeated* results and increased *efficiency* that allows us to provide both our customers and company their desired outcomes.

In every industry (but especially SaaS and cloud), learning how to properly scale customer success has been the ongoing challenge. Growing customers comes with cost pressures and profitability challenges, but increasing headcount only adds layers of management and ultimately raises costs. As a company grows, profitability declines, so you have to find ways to become more efficient.

To use a customer support example (which also has this scaling challenge), a lot of companies try many different things, but in most cases, I have found they create horrible experiences for the end user (e.g., being on hold for 45 minutes to talk to a support agent or waiting 48 hours for a ticket response). If it isn't that, you're left to deal with a chatbot, which is oftentimes far more infuriating because you aren't dealing with an actual human who's empathetic. Has this ever happened to you?

This is a challenge every company encounters as they scale. It's the job of your customer success organization to find the best practices you discovered when building your company and make them repeatable and efficient. This allows you to provide your customers with their desired outcomes, as well as hit your internal metrics.

And of course, why not deliver an amazing customer experience (CX) in the process. After all, a report by Zendesk found:

> "Roughly half of customers say they would switch to a competitor after just one bad experience. In the case of more than one bad experience, that number snowballs to 80%."[5]

So, yeah, let's do CX right!

WHAT IS CUSTOMER SUCCESS OPERATIONS?

It's not easy to gather, learn, and deploy information to get everyone on the same page (trust me), and it's especially hard when we have to handle exceptions that haven't been defined. That's why operationalizing customer success takes operational support.

Most businesses have sales ops, marketing ops, dev ops, and tech ops, so why are CS Ops roles the last to be added? I've seen companies hire CSM after CSM before they add a CS Ops position. They'll add CSMs before they add CS Ops to the team, and before management knows it, they're in trouble. "This is costly and difficult. We're

---

5   "Zendesk Customer Experience Trends Report 2020," Zendesk, 2020, https://
     d1eipm3vz4ohyo.cloudfront.net/images/blog/PR-016008_Zendesk_CX%20Trends%20
     Report%202020_Final.pdf.

having uneven results and we need to operationalize, but there is no one on the team who has that skill or capability."

For this reason, I would argue that one of the very first hires you make for your customer success organization should be in CS Ops. If you do, you will start to operationalize your business in a small but gradual way, right from square one. You will lay down the foundation of your customer success organization so that when the time comes to put your foot down and operationalize in a *big* way—hopefully, due to significant growth in your company—it will be easier and run more smoothly.

HOW WELL DO YOU KNOW YOUR CUSTOMER?

Operationalizing customer success is about taking the highly intelligent programs and processes, strategies and ideas, and using them to create actionable, useful, and impactful value for your customers. It's also about capturing momentum and inspiring your customer's motivation to expand the products they use and advocate for your company.

Finally, it means knowing when you, as a customer success leader, and/or other company leader needs to get involved to avoid a horrific crash, like stopping your customers from hurting themselves by making bad decisions or doing the wrong thing. When we operationalize customer success, we know when to get involved, how to get involved, and just how involved we should be.

Is it more appropriate to get on a plane to travel to a customer site and hold a crisis meeting, or send an email? Okay, maybe that example is a little extreme, but we need to know when a Google Meet will work as a customer communication tool versus an automated system. Operationalizing customer success means knowing when to get involved and what knowledge to deploy. It's about having enough experience to understand the situation and know what the intervention should look like.

In order to do that, first and foremost, you need to understand your customer, what the customer success criteria are, and the processes established to deliver on the promise made to the customer. Next, we need to understand how to repeatedly execute our best practices and consistently handle exceptions. Finally, we need to ensure everyone on our customer success team knows how and when to get involved as well.

HOW CAN OUR TOOLBOX HELP?

How can our toolbox help with operationalizing customer success? By using the tools inside it. When we work with the tools to stream-line best practices and scale, we operationalize customer success, allowing us to deliver our best practices in a consistent and scalable way.

It's critical we start to leverage the toolbox as soon as possible in our customer success organization to accelerate our ability to deliver successful customer outcomes every time. Having said that, if you deploy only three tools to begin your operationalizing of customer success journey, you should go with:

1. MOMENTS OF TRUTH (CUSTOMER JOURNEY MAP)
As mentioned earlier, moments of truth are tiny little interactions that happen along the customer journey. Doing the journey map exercise early in the creation of your customer success organization

will allow you to identify the moments of truth you want to nail early on. For customer success teams that are mature and have a customer journey map already created (with moments of truth identified), ask yourself, "When was the last time we updated this? Maybe it's time to do it all again."

And remember, moments of truth can be digital, off-line, or in person. Let's capture them all.

2. PLAYBOOKS

Playbooks are the heart and soul of the first pillar because they are the tools used to scale your customer success organization.

3. CUSTOMER SUCCESS PLANS

When you begin to operationalize your customer success function, you need to understand when the team is needed (moments of truth), what to do when they're needed (playbooks), and a map on how to achieve the customer's desired outcome (Customer Success Plan).

INTRODUCING DIGITAL CUSTOMER SUCCESS

Building a customer success team for scale is something we all have to do—eventually. But customer success, in its current form, simply can't scale. It's a broken approach we take today, which I believe we will remedy within the next decade. Hear me out on this.

If you are a $20 million ARR company with one customer, putting a CSM on that account is easy. It's not too expensive and pays for itself many times over. Now, if you are a $20 million

ARR company but you have 200 customers, putting a unique CSM on each of those accounts is simply not affordable. So you end up giving multiple accounts to each CSM, which reduces the potential impact the CSM can make due to time requirements needed for their portfolio of accounts. Eventually, you don't have enough CSMs to cover all the accounts (usually the long tail of accounts), and the default position is to flip them over to tech touch. Now, (typically) smaller customers will never receive the personalized, empathetic experience of your CSM team, and we may never really develop that account to its full ARR potential. So now the best of customer success is enjoyed by only a smaller, lucky few customers, rather than by all.

Don't get me wrong, this is the world we live in today. To build out a scaled customer success organization (delivering personalized journeys at scale), understanding how to automate, deploy, and analyze data will determine how well you can deliver. That's what makes this pillar so critical to customer success at scale. And because the use of data and systems is critical to gain this scale, I refer to it as digital customer success. It does not mean tech touch—humans are still very important in customer success because empathy is what drives the best outcomes. So how can you introduce humans into a technology-based delivery platform?

One example of how this could be introduced to your customer base is through the actual product itself. The only true way to scale to every single user of your solution is to deliver the service through the solution—not by sending mass emails or directing people to the community (these are valid and useful capabilities today and should be deployed) but by using the actual system your users are leveraging. It's the only answer. Human interaction can be the delivery of outcome-based services through the product at the exact time of need. This is a dream we need to deliver on. Couple this with traditional high- and mid-touch CSMs, scaling the impact of customer success can be realized.

So if you take the definition of operationalizing customer success at the beginning of the chapter, it holds just as true for digital customer success. Although tech touch and the use of systems such as marketing automation and customer success platforms have allowed us to communicate and influence in a scaled way, digital customer success allows us to directly insert human touch in a hyperscaled way. Someone way smarter than me will solve this for all of us. In fact, I am aware of an initiative underway right now that may solve this challenge. (I have a feeling you'll be hearing more about this initiative very soon in my next book, coauthored with Tiffany Powell and Brian Tucker.)

THOUGHT LEADERSHIP SERIES: BRIAN LAFAILLE

For this thought leadership piece, I asked a fellow Top 100 Customer Success Strategist *his thoughts on scaling customer success.* And true to form, **Brian LaFaille, Head of Customer Success Scale Programs (SaaS), Google Cloud,** *doesn't try to mail it in with the tired "tech touch" spiel. Through a digital lens, he delivers a thoughtful piece around the human-first experience, which is what the future will require for success at scale.*

SCALING CUSTOMER SUCCESS

BRANDS AND EMOTIONS: MOMENTS OF TRUTH MATTER

Moments of truth are when a brand manages to make a real emotional connection with a customer. These moments are the bread and butter of B2C brands such as Apple, Spotify, and Fitbit who cater to their users through a multichannel approach that utilizes email, native apps, instant chat, websites, social media, videos, still imagery, and even in-product messaging. They make moments on the user journey unique, memorable, and engaging. Think of Spotify's "Year in Review" that more than 150 million subscribers look forward to every year.

Within the next decade, B2B approaches to customer success will emphasize the multichannel system of meeting users where they are in the format that resonates most.

Intimate customer relationships are relatively easy to maintain when your customers number in the hundreds and you have a named CSM on a small portfolio of customers. However, replicating that white glove experience that adds the special, memorable moments to a customer's experience is much more difficult when customers number in the thousands or even millions, where a CSM may not be assigned.

As customer bases grow, approaches to customer success have to evolve to try and maintain these moments of truth as much as possible.

THE CONVERGENCE OF PRODUCT AND CUSTOMER SUCCESS TEAMS

Part of the evolution and maturity of customer success is the convergence of how customer success teams and product teams work.

Product teams employ strategies like A/B testing, for example, and customer success teams have adopted some of these tactics as they evaluate the various ways to keep a human element in their customer relations while communicating with an ever-growing number of customers.

This blurring of product and customer success is evident in software such as Pendo or Gainsight's PX. Ostensibly for product development, they use what would usually be considered customer success tools to help companies create better products and listen to their users' feedback.

For example, Pendo promises to help companies:

- communicate with customers better by moving communication to within their products rather than via email;
- combine product engagement, surveys, and feedback to maximize customer retention; and
- optimize trial conversions and user onboarding in-product.

All these features aim to improve the customer experience by developing a better product that builds customer communication directly into the product itself, thus increasing user sentiment.

PUTTING IT INTO PRACTICE

Scaling moments of truth to an ever-increasing customer base means studying your user's behavior and applying the right channel to the right user in the right moment.

Here's how to think about blending a product management approach with customer success to improve and scale your customer experience.

1. **Define customer behaviors:** Behavioral mapping is a research tool used to record the behaviors of individuals in situations. It's a process product teams leverage when developing new product lines or features. And, in this first phase, it's all about defining what critical user behaviors are seen in successful customers. By defining these behaviors, you can map out the user's critical user behavior milestones needed to receive value from your platform. These behaviors have a few characteristics. First, they're time-bound—they need to be seen in a certain amount of time. Next, these user behaviors need to be quantifiable. That is, they need to be measured. Last, these behaviors should be agreed upon by a cross-functional team of customer-facing departments (sales, customer success, support, etc.).

2. **Define measures of success:** Once your user behaviors are defined, consider setting measurable targets for increasing the certain high-impact, high-value behaviors that lead to retention and expansion. Having quantifiable and proactive measures of success ensures your team focuses on driving the right in-product behaviors that lead to value creation for the customer and retention for you and your company.

3. **Develop communication channels:** With key user behaviors defined and measurable targets established, it's time to think about how you can influence those behaviors with new and innovative digital channels. A robust multichannel approach leverages text, imagery, in-app, community, webinar, and video. If you have one or more of these channels already established, consider evaluating its effectiveness in driving the key behaviors you've identified. If you're just getting started, pick a new channel and start to think through how that new channel can embellish the CSM experience you have today. Remember, digital success does not mean tech touch. These channels are meant to embellish and extend your customer success experience for your customer base.

4. **Test, iterate, improve, and add channels over time:** With one or more of these new digital channels established, create time to evaluate channel performance in two dimensions.

   - Is the channel resonating with your users? You can monitor that through channel engagement rates (click-through rate, open rate, etc.).
   - Is the channel driving the key user behaviors (as done through A/B testing with a control group and test group who receives these new channels)?

To achieve the best possible customer success experience, a digital-first and CSM supplemented approach is key in the next decade. Define the key behaviors that lead to retention and expansion, establish measurable product-oriented targets, then test and iterate new digital channels over time. The next customer success decade will lead with digital channels and supplement with one-on-one interactions (where it makes sense) to extend your customer success team's reach and enhance the value your customers receive from your platform.

ADD VALUE AND LEAD THEM HOME

Like my grandparents teaching me the skills to survive in the bush, operationalizing customer success is about teaching your customer success team the skills they need to find their way home and add value to your customers. Now that you know how to organize your operations, let's dive into Pillar #2: Onboarding, where you'll learn how to bring customers in.

CHAPTER 4

———

PILLAR #2: ONBOARDING

"VALUE DEFINED"

The Seven Customer Success Pillars

Customer Journey Lifecycle Stages

Operationalize CS · Onboarding · Adoption · Retention · Expansion · Advocacy · Strategic Advisor

www.cspillars.com

Track and field is one of my favorite events at the summer Olympics. I especially love the hurdles.

At the games in Rio in 2016, a Fort Lauderdale-born athlete named Jeffrey Julmis was running the 110-meter hurdles for his native country, Haiti. He had competed well enough in the quarterfinals and had advanced to the semifinals.

Shortly after the race began, Julmis misjudged his spacing and tripped over the first hurdle. His arms and legs went flying, and when they made contact with the ground, they were all tangled up in the same hurdle that had done him in. Needless to say, because he tripped over the first hurdle, he didn't qualify for the finals. His Olympic adventure had suddenly ended.

Maybe you were expecting a winning and uplifting story; well, welcome to the world of customer success. It's a tough function to be in, but that makes the victories that much sweeter.

The purpose of the story was to simply say a poor onboarding experience is like tripping over the first hurdle. It turns the entire journey into a game of catch-up rather than a game of leadership. If you can't get onboarding right, how do you expect to turn customers into advocates and ambassadors, which is an important goal? To ensure our entire customer's journey is a success, we have to nail onboarding right out of the gate.

In this chapter, we're going to talk about onboarding, the pillar with the biggest influence on whether your customer decides to renew that first year. If your customer has a bad onboarding experience, you may think you have time to fix the relationship before they decide to renew, but you're wrong. When it comes to the customer journey, tripping over the first hurdle (onboarding) is extremely difficult to recover from.

But what is customer onboarding? What does it look like? And why is it so critical?

TELL ME MORE, TELL ME MORE (ABOUT ONBOARDING)

Customer onboarding is a fundamental step on your customer's journey, so let's define it.

> *Customer onboarding is jointly defining a Customer Success Plan together and proactively guiding a customer to achieve value one in the fastest possible time.*

That's a mouthful, I know, so let's break the sentence down.

We are the experts and we have been hired to provide value. We want to *proactively guide the customer* through the onboarding process and lead them through our proven best practices.

Your new customers don't know how to work with the different functions inside your company and use your product to transform their organization. More than likely, they've never worked with you or your solution before.

But you have. You probably use your product every day. All you do is use your product (well, maybe that isn't *all* you do, but you get the point), so it's your job to find ways to lead the customer to success.

This map is called a Customer Success Plan (a tool in our toolbox). Onboarding is the moment on the customer's journey when we can sit with the customer and confirm what we've learned from the sales handoff (or prior), ensure alignment around goals and milestones, reset expectations where there is confusion, and ultimately map out the Customer Success Plan with the customer.

Next, we want the customer to clear that hurdle and have their first win—*achieve value one.*

Their first business achievement solidifies the customer's decision to purchase your solution. They think, *We chose the right product. We're with the right vendor. They know what they're doing because we've already seen value.*

During onboarding, you want to give your customer something they care about and value, so you need to sit down with them and agree on what value one should look like. Agree on a win your customer can share with their management that will help them (and your company) look good.

Now, to be clear, the customer will likely have value two, three, four, and even five (note: value one is not always their desired outcome but rather a step toward that outcome), but your job in onboarding is to focus solely on value one.

DIFFERENT TYPES OF VALUE ONE

Both the customer and CSM measure success with the value one metric during onboarding. Typically, there are three different types.

1. USE CASE

This is a specific way the solution can potentially be used. A customer may think, *Wouldn't it be incredible if we could do X?*

They then research products and decide to go with yours. Your goal, your value one, is to help them achieve X.

2. DESIRED STATE

This is an environment or a state the customer lives in. It doesn't hit a specific metric but creates an environment that helps the customer move forward. Maybe there is massive confusion as to who does what on a specific project. Perhaps it's as simple as to roll out the software so everyone is clear on their individual roles. I've seen desired state used at several previous companies but sparingly. Of all the value one types, it's probably the least used, but it is still relevant.

3. DEFINED VALUE

This one is straightforward. It's about hitting a specific and defined metric. If the customer wants to have the internal infrastructure set up to begin deployment by a certain date, that's value one. If the customer wants to reach a certain number of internal named users of the solution in a proof of concept in a certain time frame, *that's* value one.

No matter which value one type you choose, make sure it's captured and defined in the Customer Success Plan. It's essential everyone be on the same page, so record those details.

VALUE ONE SHOULD BE ACHIEVABLE

Value one should be achievable by the CSM. For example, if you identify a value one that's impossible to achieve early on, you're setting yourself up to fail.

I once worked with an aerospace company on an airport software implementation project. The value one they set during the presale cycle was the "successful rollout and deployment of all new systems across all the airports they managed," a metric that would take 18 months to complete.

How do you deliver value quickly on an 18-month project? When things go wrong, the customer will first lose heart, then lose faith. Competitors will come in next, and the whole project will get derailed because there was no early win.

In this particular circumstance, we were able to identify there was a risk to achieving value one, so we proactively got in front of it to remove it as a high hurdle to success. As an alternative, we suggested a much more feasible, attainable value one. We suggested the "successful rollout and deployment of all new systems inside one airport." I explained this was a better value one because it would be a joint win early on. It would also give us a chance to work out the kinks and fine-tune our processes before we rolled it out across multiple countries.

My customer's response? "Yeah, that makes more sense!"

DELIVER VALUE QUICKLY

It is of the utmost importance that the customer and the CSM agree to and jointly own the defined value one. It's also crucial to deliver on that value in the *fastest time possible*—the last part of our definition of onboarding.

In the SaaS world, customers pay for use of your product or service monthly, so they need to see a fast win. If they pay you for six months without seeing any value, they'll think they wasted their money and feel frustrated.

Customers don't pay us for our service or our product; they are paying us for the value those things provide. Customers pay us for the outcomes, so we need to provide a *positive* outcome quickly. We also want to give them a quick win because we want to move them into the next phase of their customer journey—adoption.

During onboarding, we are mainly responsible for three things: guiding the customer (through a Customer Success Plan), achieving value one, and doing it quickly.

ONBOARDING VERSUS ADOPTION

Customer onboarding is a crucial step in your customer's journey. Why is it so crucial? Because it's your first opportunity to provide your customer with value.

The number one reason customers churn is because they don't see the value that was promised or desired. They don't leave because it's a bad product fit or there's a competitor that offered them a lower rate. If your customer is seeing value right out of the gate, they won't bother to look for competitors.

We have to nail onboarding, and when we do, we have to do it exceptionally. As I've said before, it's the first hurdle on our customer's journey with us; we can't trip over it.

Exceptional onboarding includes a few key elements (and I'm going to tell you all about them), but before we get into that, let's quickly address the elephant in the room.

Some of you reading this are probably thinking, *What's the difference between customer onboarding and customer adoption? Aren't they the same thing?*

If this is you, you're not alone. Many of the people I talk to often confuse onboarding with adoption (which is understandable because the two often meld together), and when I talk to company leaders about their new client onboarding and adoption best practices, I regularly hear, "We roll out the software and get it up and running, and then train all the users."

But onboarding and adoption aren't the same—not even close.

ONBOARDING

For the sake of clarification, let's take a moment to get on the same page and define the differences between the two—at least the way I see it.

Onboarding is a finite activity: it's the definitive period of time when the customer gets to know you. The customer also learns how to use your company's support system, leverage documentation, and whom to contact if they need any help. They get to establish a Customer Success Plan that maps out the journey in agreement with the CSM.

The onboarding period typically includes the deployment of technology. In the SaaS world, that can happen in as little as one day or take as long as a few months.

For example, when you sign up for a free Gmail account, you receive access to your new inbox in a matter of minutes—onboarding really is that simple!

Regardless of whether your company's onboarding process is short or long, the process has a definitive end date. There will come a point when you will say, "Okay, we have onboarded this customer successfully. Now we need to focus on widespread adoption of our provided solution."

When we think of onboarding, we always think of new customer logos only, and onboarding them when the contracts have been signed.

But onboarding can happen several times throughout a customer's journey with you. Say you originally sold your product to the finance department, and now the marketing department wants to start using it, too. The marketing team has no idea how to use your product or services (such as support), so they need to be onboarded.

Or maybe you're introducing a new product. Your customer doesn't know how to use it, so you're going to have to onboard them. Yes, hard to believe but it's still onboarding.

Onboarding can happen several times for the same logo, but each onboarding event has a clear beginning, middle, and end.

ADOPTION

Adoption, on the other hand, never stops. We'll discuss the how-to of adoption fully in the next chapter. For now, the difference, as I see it, is that adoption is ongoing and ever present. There will always be people inside the organization who don't know everything your software has to offer. These could be new employees or even existing ones who aren't familiar with the product yet.

And in the SaaS world in particular, new features and new versions will be rolled out constantly. As many of you reading this already know, new features and/or software versions are often released quarterly, monthly, or even weekly, which requires ongoing training and troubleshooting. Adoption is the process of getting your customers to *adopt* the new features that just came out for your product.

In summary, adoption is ongoing, whereas onboarding is finite.

TIPS AND TRICKS FOR ONBOARDING

Onboarding impacts the entire customer journey experience—getting off on the right foot as it were. I've come up with five simple steps that create exceptional onboarding:

1. **Focus on the Right People:** Before the onboarding process begins, we need to know whom (on the customer's side) we need to focus on. Who are the right people? Who are the stakeholders? The right people could be project managers, administrators, developers, or the customer's CSMs.
2. **Understand the Specific Goals of the Right Individuals:** Once we know whom to focus on, we need to understand their goals. What are they trying to achieve? How soon are they trying to achieve it? How can we make them look good?
3. **Clear Timelines and Execution Plans:** Now that you know whom to focus on and what their goals are, you need to figure out how to execute. What does onboarding for this customer look like? Is the launch going to be small and sent out to a pilot group of customers? Or is the launch going to be massive and rolled out to 10,000 customers on the same day? Set clear timelines you both agree to (and you can manage).

4. **Understand and Deliver on Value One:** I can't reiterate the importance of value one enough. Customers churn when they don't see value. Delivering on value one quickly is the best way to provide an exceptional onboarding experience.

5. **Understand the Path to Maturity after Launch (aka Customer Success Plan):** Chess is a game of strategy, and onboarding is no different. You need to always be thinking several moves ahead so you can understand how the customer can effectively use your product or service to transform their business. How can the client best use this technology to transition into a successful product adoption? The Customer Success Plan is designed to help you navigate this.

A CSM is like a customer's guide. By following these steps to exceptional onboarding, they guide the customer up and down the mountain and through rough onboarding terrain and beyond. This should be easy for the CSM because they are familiar with the landscape—they've trekked through it a million times.

CSM—THE *EASY* BUTTON

A CSM's job is to guide the customer through the onboarding process. Their job is also to make it not only exceptional but also easy.

Making the customer experience easy is paramount throughout the customer journey and particularly so during onboarding. If the process is too hard and too painful, you might lose the customer before they even have a chance to begin.

Let me give you some tips for creating an easy onboarding experience.

EXPLODE OUT OF THE GATE

First, we need to start early. When it comes to implementation, we need to begin the work we're doing with our customers as soon as possible. Don't wait until the project has been live for two months to create a Customer Success Plan. You need to get started on it at the beginning of the engagement. Days (but no more than a week) after the contract has been signed, start building your customer's plan. This will make it easy for your customer to begin their customer journey with you and start using your product.

As a bonus, getting started on a Customer Success Plan early will separate you from the pack because most companies focus all their resources on the technical aspects of the implementation. They're too focused on the logistics of project delivery rather than the long-term customer goals. When you start your Customer Success Plan early, you have time to talk to your customer about the long-term success of the project. You have time to focus on the future.

REMOVE OBSTACLES

Next, you need to remove obstacles. Once the Customer Success Plan has been created, review it to determine anything that may stand in the way of a successful onboarding experience. Proactively look at how other customers have gone through the process so you can find potential problems and get in front of them. For example, if you see a lot of customers falling off in the early stages of onboarding because IT needs three weeks for implementation preparation, you know you need to start the process earlier to avoid the frustrating delay. Removing obstacles will make the onboarding experience easier for your customer.

LEARN TO LISTEN

Third, you have to learn to listen. It's natural to do a lot of talking when first onboarding a customer because the customer has no idea what to do. They are looking for you to help guide them, but that doesn't mean you should do all the talking. Listening to your customer is a preeminent element of a strong customer success philosophy, so don't forget to do it during onboarding. Ask questions and really listen to your customer's answers.

Listen to your competition, too. Your customer is getting hit from all sides—social media, marketing, advertising, the competition, their peers, and your company—and knowing what your competition is saying can help you see things from your customer's perspective. When you do, you are learning and understanding details that may shift your sentiment on certain priorities. This new perspective will also help you navigate the customer's future. Hey, Blockbuster, did you listen to how Netflix took care of your customers?

HOW CAN OUR TOOLBOX HELP?

We now know how to make onboarding easy and exceptional, but how do we create an effective onboarding strategy? In the following, I'll show you how our toolbox can help.

MOMENTS OF TRUTH

Onboarding is flooded with moments of truth—the series of interactions between the customer and your company. There are welcome emails, kickoff calls, product deployment, and a number of other touch points where you contact your customer. A welcome email, for example, is an autogenerated email sent to new customers to invite them to use the software. Typically, these types of emails are in Times New Roman and start with a basic, nondescript, "Hello. You have been invited to log in to a new platform." It's impersonal, it borders on looking like spam, and it often doesn't welcome the customer in a warm, fuzzy way that makes them happy they chose yours.

As customer success professionals, it's our job to make the customer experience easier and less threatening to consume new information. Instead of sending a boring, obviously automated welcome email, create an HTML email that's personalized. You could include a short video explaining (in a fun way) how the software works or even a case study from another customer who has seen immense value from the product.

In this example, it's likely that the customer success function doesn't own the welcome email process—the product or marketing teams do. You should lobby for the customer's best interests anyway because it's your job to make sure the customer has the best experience possible.

PLAYBOOKS

Moments of truth trigger the need for playbooks, meaning any of the pillars could have a million different playbooks. When deciding which playbook to build first, pick one that will have the largest impact on a broader set of customers—for example, the welcome email in our previous example.

Don't build a playbook you will never use. Instead, develop one for a moment of truth within your control and your ability to execute. Create your first playbooks where you own the resources, the infrastructure, and the collateral.

CUSTOMER SUCCESS PLAN

As mentioned, a Customer Success Plan should be started within days after a customer signs the contract, and within the plan, there should be an onboarding outline so both the CSM and the customer know what to expect and how to measure success. Customer Success Plans require a lot of careful planning attention to detail specific to the customer.

Customer Success Plans should include your customer's desired outcomes and value milestones. The Customer Success Plan illustrates how both you and the customer define success, and in regard to onboarding, it should include value one.

CUSTOMER HEALTH

Customer health is another tool you should utilize during onboarding. The main purpose of utilizing the customer health tool during onboarding is to understand how your customer health score is measured and so you know what to focus on during adoption, the next pillar.

Remember, we typically use six questions to determine customer health, but before you start to calculate your health score for onboarding, take a step back. Which inputs are pivotal during onboarding? Which aren't?

When calculating your health score during onboarding, you want to keep in mind that no one is using the product yet. When you finish onboarding, a few people will be using it, but the number will still be small. Thus, the weighting of adoption should be lower during onboarding than other stages of the customer life cycle.

CUSTOMER RISK

With customers, there are always risks, but there are two risks that are especially threatening during onboarding: launch risk and adoption risk.

- **Launch risk:** Launch risk happens when a project gets stalled or has a red or yellow risk assessment (as if it's in trouble). The problem with launch risk is that it delays value attainment—it prevents our customer from seeing value as quickly as possible. This most commonly happens when customer success doesn't do a good job of letting the customer know (up front) everything they need to execute quickly (such as access to databases, technology, or people). If we don't do a good job informing them, we're going to be in trouble.

- **Adoption risk:** Adoption risk takes place during the Adoption Pillar but is set in motion during onboarding. Poor onboarding leads to poor adoption. Risks are everywhere. Define a risk mitigation approach—and make a playbook—so when there's a problem, you know how to fix it. Successful onboarding is all about making it easy for your customer, right?

SEGMENTATION

Segmentation will help you categorize your customers. In the case of onboarding, you want to know whether your new customer is going to be low touch or high touch.

- **Low touch:** If the onboarding event is for the new user of an existing customer and doesn't require a lot of effort, the customer is low touch. Or if you have a million different users but use a self-service onboarding training (because you obviously can't train that many users, individually, yourself), that customer is low touch, too. Low-touch onboarding best practices are designed to scale.
- **High touch:** High-touch customers, on the other hand, require white glove onboarding. If your product will significantly change your new customer's workflow, chances are, the onboarding process is going to be complex and slow. That's high touch. If your customer is immature and had never used your type of technology before, they usually will be high touch, too, and will likely need an extensive implementation process. High touch isn't hand-holding, but it *does* ensure customers keep up with the steady stream of knowledge they need to capture in order to have success with your product.

THOUGHT LEADERSHIP SERIES: GARY LUTON

*I asked **Gary Luton, SVP of Customer Success at Trip Actions,** what his thoughts were around onboarding, including the sales handover moment. I got to see Gary's skills and capabilities while working together at Salesforce back in the day. Sharing his insight and perspective will hopefully add more to your body of knowledge around onboarding.*

ONBOARDING: BUILDING THE FOUNDATION

Onboarding is one of the most important phases in a customer life cycle.

If done right, onboarding will set you and your customer up for a great relationship—they will become a customer for life. If done poorly, it can result in a customer not getting value and then not remaining a customer for very long.

You have already spent many hours in the sales cycle convincing your customer you have the best product or service and that you can provide a solution better than your competitors. This is the stage in the customer life cycle where trust and expectations are the highest, and now is your time to show you can live up to those claims.

Of course, not all onboarding is the same. Depending on the product or service, onboarding a customer can be a simple process that takes a matter of minutes, or it could be much more in depth and last for days or even longer.

One thing that is clear is that the onboarding process is unlikely to deliver a lot of real direct value for the customer, so it is important that customers are onboarded as quickly and as effectively as possible. This focus on "time to value" is critical for all SaaS companies where customer success and value over the term is important for retention.

With customer success in mind, there are four things that need to be in place for successful onboarding:

1. Good sales handover
2. Clear customer goals and objectives
3. A well-defined process
4. Clear communication

It is likely the person who will onboard the customer is different than the salesperson. Therefore, it is important there is an effective and frictionless handover between the salesperson and the success resource. How many times have you been frustrated because you've been passed on the phone from person to person, and the new person did not know anything about the previous conversations?

Poor handovers between team members erode trust and reduce customer confidence, and you need both to successfully onboard a customer. This handover is best performed in person and supported by a good customer relationship system that can be used as your single system of record for all your customer data.

As part of this handover, it is important you understand your customer's goals, objectives, and reasons for choosing your solution in the first place. Your customer's rationale for choosing your solution should serve as a compass during the onboarding process and the entire life of the customer relationship.

If the sales cycle has been executed well, then you likely already know the goals and objectives the customer is trying to achieve. You should use the onboarding process to validate these expectations and explain again how your solution will help.

A clear and well-defined onboarding process is also important for you and your customer. You should set expectations in terms of outcomes, duration, and effort. Clear roles and responsibilities on both sides will help ensure that time is not wasted in the process—a customer that onboards effectively will be able to achieve the best possible time to value. Many onboarding processes fail when expectations are not clearly set and roles and responsibilities are not well defined.

As you go through the onboarding process, there should be clear and frequent communication between you and your customer. Use regular communication to continue to reinforce expectations and hold everyone accountable to the timeline and process that you've outlined.

Finally, when you complete the onboarding stage, you should communicate the stage is complete, explain the process from there, and check with your customer if anything has been left outstanding.

Onboarding serves as the foundation for your long-term relationship. Like any foundation, if built solidly, it will serve you well through your customer journey.

PLAY A GAME OF FOLLOW-THE-LEADER

Successful onboarding proactively guides the customer and helps them realize value one as quickly as possible. That means you need to first focus on the right individuals (who are the stakeholders?) and understand their goals. You then need to create clear timelines and understand how to deliver on value one and, finally, understand the path to adoption and maturity after launch. The Customer Success Plan can capture this and allow you to align your customer and company on the path forward.

Onboarding is finite and concludes when you achieve value one. But if you don't nail onboarding, it's kind of like tripping over the first hurdle at the Olympics—you end up playing a game of catch-up as opposed to a game of follow-the-leader.

Nailing onboarding is essential, but it isn't complicated. Just follow the steps outlined in this chapter. Once you have successfully onboarded your customer, it's time to move to the next phase of the customer journey, adoption. We're going to cover that next.

CHAPTER 5

PILLAR #3: ADOPTION

"VALUE REALIZED"

The Seven Customer Success Pillars

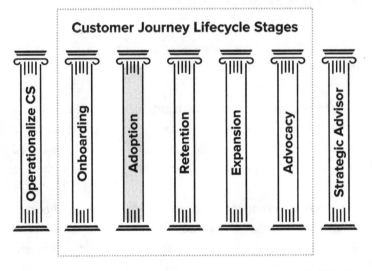

Customer Journey Lifecycle Stages

Operationalize CS | Onboarding | Adoption | Retention | Expansion | Advocacy | Strategic Advisor

www.cspillars.com

Back in 2007, my boss at the time bought me my first iPhone. He gifted one to all of his direct reports.

"This new Apple iPhone was just released this week and you should have one."

I looked at the phone and thought,

Why would I want this? I love my BlackBerry, and I can type 50 words a minute on it. It's my favorite device in the world, and you're giving me this thing that doesn't have any buttons on it and expect me to use it?

The iPhone was too different, too foreign. I had no idea how to use it, and I didn't want to learn. I didn't adopt it because I didn't know how it worked. So I gave it to my executive business partner.

QUESTIONS ABOUT ADOPTION, ANSWERED

Today, my whole life runs on an iPhone. I sleep with it, eat with it, run with it, and use it for everything. Is seems like it's in my hands 24 hours a day.

I can't remember the specific moment when I decided to bite the bullet and adopt the use of the iPhone, but when I did, my life invariably changed for the better. When I was first introduced to one, I couldn't be bothered, but today, I can't live without it.

When customers adopt your product, you want it to become something they can't live without. Better yet, they enjoy using your product. But what is adoption? If you ask ten different people to describe it, you'll get ten different answers.

"It's when everyone on the team uses the product."

"When more than 50% of the team are using the product."

"When the customer uses the product they bought."

No one seems to have a clear understanding of what successful customer adoption looks like, so I've come up with my own definition.

> *Customer adoption is achieving operational dependence, while simultaneously achieving business value by using the right features and functionality of the solution.*

We want to *achieve operational dependence* because it indicates the people who need to use this tool are using it, and the solution is being used by your customer the way it was intended to achieve value and their goals.

OPERATIONAL DEPENDENCE

I am now operationally dependent on my iPhone. I take it everywhere and use it all the time. Operational dependence means getting your customer to use your product each time because in many cases, there are alternative solutions they can likely use. For example, for video conferencing, I can think of a dozen different, perfectly capable tools right off the top of my head: for example, Google Meet, Zoom, WebEx, Skype, and Facetime. If your product is Google Meet, how do you get your customers to use it (as opposed to the other options) *every* single time, especially when IT can't lock down BYO devices (which makes options such as Facetime easy to access).

When you don't achieve operational dependence, there is a competitive risk. The users are thinking, *I don't want to use that product because I use this product and it's better and/or easier. It's also fun. It has GIFs and animations (yes, people are strangely particular when it comes to software).* When all of your customers' employees aren't using your product, it means they're using a different product. The risk is that over time, the *other* product gains traction, everyone starts to prefer it and migrate, and eventually, you get kicked out.

DEMONSTRATED BUSINESS VALUE

Successful customer adoption also means you have *simultaneously demonstrated business value.* Throughout the adoption process, you need to put forth all our efforts to attain the business outcomes the customer sought to achieve when they purchased your solution in the first place. If everyone is using the product but you aren't driving business value, your adoption plan isn't working.

ACHIEVING BUSINESS VALUE AND THE CUSTOMER'S GOALS

Basically, we need the users to be able to do what they have always done but do it more and do it better. We need to ensure features and functionality enablement has happened. Most people think adoption is license utilization, but it's more about the depth of features and functionality utilization. Is the customer using the power of your solution to achieve their business outcomes? We don't have to enable users on all features and functionality, but the CSM should identify which features are critical for success early in the deployment and get that training into the hands of the first users. True adoption can maximize the change to realizing business value and outcomes.

WHY SHOULD WE CARE ABOUT ADOPTION?

As customer success professionals, one of our number one

responsibilities is to eliminate churn, and adoption is the key lever that helps us do that.

Your success is tied to your customer's success, which is a big SaaS business model shift. Fifteen years ago, enterprise companies would purchase a $50 million implementation package with a three-year rollout period. For the vendor, if it didn't work, it didn't matter because that company already received their $50 million. They were onto the next sale. That doesn't happen in this day and age. If you don't provide value, especially during the adoption phase, the client leaves and you lose future revenue.

Customers leave when they don't see value, so providing it during the adoption process is paramount to the role of customer success. When adoption is done well, it leads to a renewal.

It also leads to customer expansion, which drives incremental sales and market valuation for your company, a key board-level metric. You're in the business to make money for your stakeholders and shareholders, so it's critical to get adoption right for future renewal and expansion opportunities.

The bottom line is, if the customer doesn't see value, they won't renew. Adoption drives retention, expansion, and a lot more (additional information on that last bit yet to come), and that's why it matters.

CSMS AND ADOPTION: A LOVE STORY

The CSM is responsible for adoption and will ultimately be held accountable for its success, but many other departments are involved, too. For example, sales sets adoption expectations during the sales process, and services runs implementation and then there's training. Marketing usually has a hand in adoption, too. By the time customer success gets involved with adoption, many other departments have already had their hands in the pot and impacted the customer's perception of value.

CSMs need to be aware of all the elements that influence adoption for your customer and help improve processes where necessary. This may mean identifying horrible "best practices" that are sending the customer in the wrong direction and having the right conversations in order to get them fixed. If the CSM is lucky enough to walk into an adoption process that is already amazing (and the team is nailing it), you may not have to change a thing. You may be able to just go with the flow.

> Ideally, you are influencing the adoption process by being involved in the presales motion (sometimes referred to as pillar #1.5).

The first thing to remember is, you aren't alone. There is an entire community of internal colleagues working toward making the customer's adoption a success, too.

GENERATE OPERATIONAL DEPENDENCE

Thinking back to our definition for adoption, CSMs are also responsible for generating operational dependence. Most B2B (business-to-business) companies rarely think about this, but B2C (business-to-consumer) companies figured this out years ago. A good example is the mobile game Candy Crush.

Candy Crush starts off simply with clear instructions (and animation) on how to play the game. "Match three objects! Move your finger from left to right and pull this piece of candy down so it lines up with two other matching pieces of candy. Boom! You've made your first match!" The game then goes on to introduce new concepts and skills slowly, level to level, to teach the customer how to use the product as it was intended. This creates operational dependence on the game. "I like this. This is easy. I know how to use it and I'm comfortable."

So how do B2B companies mirror this? How do we develop a dependency to establish new work habits and keep those habits going day after day? An example would be that most companies advise you to attend a (insert single-digit number here)-day training class to learn everything you need to know.

And more—a lot more! This is an example of misunderstanding how to get effective adoption.

It really begins when the CSM creates the Customer Success Plan and continues in onboarding, then proactively leads the customer to adoption. You need to remove any operational barriers that prevent their employees from using the system and getting value.

For example, let's say your product needs to be hooked into the back end of a database and be specifically configured, and you know customer approvals usually take one to two weeks. Even though that particular process isn't scheduled to kick off for another month, you should get involved now so everything plugs in seamlessly when the time comes.

If the customer has to wait, everything stops, and you lose momentum. If you keep everything moving forward, the customer will see value as quickly as possible.

IDENTIFY AND ENGAGE STAKEHOLDERS

CSMs need to understand what success looks like. They need to know who needs to get trained and properly enabled to use the product.

Your customer's stakeholders provide the insight you need. They usually know what success looks like and are typically the person who can make things happen internally. In order to identify the stakeholder, Shane Anastasi, Founder and CEO of PS Principles (also one of the inspirations for this book and a friend of mine from college for going on 30 years), suggests starting with these four questions:

1. Are they the budget owner?
2. Are they the signatory authority?
3. Is their job at risk if the project fails?
4. Are they the operational owner?

If you answered yes to two or more questions, it's likely that that person is a stakeholder—being a budget owner isn't enough. When I worked at Salesforce, I had my own budget and could approve anything up to $250,000, but anything more than that needed to be signed directly by the CFO. For larger investments, I wasn't the only stakeholder; the CFO was, too.

CONSUMPTION AND WIDESPREAD ADOPTION

CSMs must take the responsibility for monitoring consumption, including software, number of hours of services consumed, bandwidth taken up, application programming interface (API) calls, even support packages that have been purchased—consumption isn't limited to just licenses. Companies purchase a certain capacity from you as a vender, and you need to make sure they maximize it, or the customer will likely question the service when it's time to renew. It's like paying for HBO and Showtime when you watch only HGTV and Bravo TV (hmm, a very American-centric comment. So for any Aussies reading this, think of *Kath & Kim* or *House Rules*). The point is, we need to make sure your customer consumes everything they're purchasing.

CSMs are also responsible for widespread adoption. Is your customer using the product the right way? Are they utilizing all the features available to make their jobs easier? In the cloud world, we potentially have access to a plethora of usage data, so it's easy to see how many people are logging in, how often they log in, what they're doing while they're logged in, and so forth. Your customer's stats offer great insight as to where additional adoption efforts are needed.

A "ride along" can provide the best information about how your customer is using the product. Go to their offices and sit with them for a day to watch how they use it (outside of a pandemic, of course). Often, you'll find out they aren't utilizing the product the way it was intended. This insight can give you ideas about new features or alternative adoption strategies; it will also tell you if the customer is moving in the right direction.

I think a good CSM would take it a step further and hold "office hours" regularly. Visit your customer's office, bring in food, and open yourself up to user questions and feedback. Or do something virtual and spice it up with some cool online icebreakers.

Ask them, "What do you love? What do you hate? What do you wish it could do? Which feature did you just discover and wish you had known about sooner?"

User feedback is a great opportunity for your customer to have a voice and for you to share that voice with your internal team.

RELEASE READINESS AND FEATURED FEATURES

When a new feature or product is released, the CSM needs to be ready to sit down with the customer and explain it. They should be ready to recommend a feature that would be great for the customer. Release readiness reinforces operational dependence and drives business value.

CSMs should also know what makes their product unique and sticky as well as their product's competitive differentiator. And they should be able to promote it like crazy. A CSM should make sure everyone, especially the stakeholder, knows why the feature is amazing and why they should be using it. The more your customers fall in love with your product's capabilities, the more they'll build operational dependence that you can leverage for renewals and upselling.

And for scale customers, record these information sessions for distribution, or better yet, deliver webinars to allow customers to ask questions.

LEAD ADOPTION

In order to lead adoption, the CSM must first change the user's behavior (through the use of your software). That's hard to do. There are entire companies that exist to support change management initiatives. It's imperative that all CSMs are enabled on change management strategies—investing in training is paramount to arming the CSMs with the tools needed to guide this process (typically, they are not leading it, but they should have a heavy influence on the change management program). CSMs should provide insights, playbooks, and assets for the change management program being used. Better yet, monetize change management as a success service (more on that later in the book).

Changing a user's behavior is difficult, but it's not impossible. When getting someone to change, you have to make them understand why your product can make them more successful than other solutions. A key part of leading adoption is evangelizing why your solution beats the solution they currently have in place from a value perspective.

Then you need to bury the FUD (fear, uncertainty, and doubt) by making it easy for them to switch. Maybe you provide them with a cheat sheet? Or you could work with marketing to create a video or reference card with training tips that translate easily for the user.

Remember, you aren't the only one involved in the customer's adoption of your product (we talked about this already), but it is your responsibility to lead it and create more value.

BEST PRACTICE BENCHMARKS

Most people (especially here in the United States) like to compare themselves to others. We do it on social media and on the SATs. We also compare where we went to school and which sports teams we like. Culturally, it's a part of our DNA.

CSMs are responsible to help build best practice benchmarks and showing a customer how they compare to others in their industry in terms of maturity, sophistication, and value attainment. When you do, it motivates them to believe *We can do better!*

If your customer is more successful than their competitors, you can help them leverage that benchmark data to better promote their own company. The more you help here, the more value you generate for your customers.

CUSTOMER FEEDBACK

As you now know, your customer is constantly providing your company with feedback. As a CSM, it is your responsibility to proactively gather that feedback and act on it.

Is the customer seeing value from the product? Are the customer's employees adopting the product? If you get a lot of noes, that's a red flag that you aren't creating operational dependence and you aren't driving value.

Just remember to act on the feedback—I can't emphasize this enough! If a customer has something to say and it isn't being heard, that's a red flag to them and to you.

MILESTONES

Finally, a CSM develops milestones to reach the desired outcome. These are different than KPIs. KPIs measure how good you're doing at any given time, whereas milestones are parts of the customer success journey broken into key sections.

Creating and monitoring milestones will allow you to determine whether you and the customer are on the right track. The milestones will vary depending on your customer's desired outcomes, but it's necessary to set them to determine whether the project is on track.

Let's say that value one is to get a department of 50 people to use your new software platform within 90 days. Between you and the customer, a map of milestones (with dates) can be determined to achieve that outcome.

- **Milestone 1:** Create awareness of the new platform with the department in question (don't forget to include the "What's in it for me?" component). A fun video is a good idea here.
- **Milestone 2:** Establish some internal champions within the customer base to help with the adoption.
- **Milestone 3:** Formal training program rolled out to users (don't forget the "This is how we used to do it; now this is how we will do it" in conjunction with the feature/functionality training).
- **Milestone 4:** Review daily active users or monthly active users (or desired metrics for success).
- **Milestone 5:** How deep are the users on the features/functionality of the solution, as it pertains to achieving business value.

Although this is a simplistic example, it allows you to measure the progress toward the desired outcome through milestones and dates.

Here's a little trick of the trade: I suggest asking your customer directly if they will be a reference for your company during the adoption phase. Yep, before they have even rolled out the software broadly or received a ton of value. Although securing a reference this early would be cool, what you're actually looking for is a red flag.

If they say, "Absolutely," you have achieved a significant milestone. Their acceptance indicates a certain level of satisfaction they have with you as the CSM, the implementation team, the sales team (and the product team and services team), and the brand in general in the early stages of the relationship. This is a great indicator of how well you've executed the presales, onboarding, and adoption pieces of the customer's journey.

However, if the customer doesn't say yes, that's a flag. If you hear, "No, I don't think so. We're still in the early stages. Let's see how everything plays out," you may have a problem brewing. You must ensure you do a survey at this point to assess the customer's experience so far. We need to see what (if anything) we could have improved on to ensure our playbooks and team are aligned on the best practices needed to create a great customer experience.

It also means you may not be creating company champions. Most adoption happens from inside the customer's organization: "Check out this new software I'm using. Have you seen it? I use it all the time and it #ROCKS." If your customer turns down your reference request, you are already delaying the creation of champions and advocates.

Company champions drive engagement throughout the entire organization and create a circle of influence. CSMs have to figure out how to foster and nurture company champions and make sure they feel supported during the adoption process. When they do, you can start to build (and harness) a groundswell of enthusiasm within your customer's organization.

Once adoption is complete and the customer sees value, you can ask if they'd like to share their success story in a case study.

If they say yes, that's another great milestone for a CSM because it indicates customer satisfaction and a job well done.

HOW CAN OUR TOOLBOX HELP?

Adoption, as presented in this chapter, can be distilled into three phases:

1. Define the path to success.
2. Understand KPIs, value metrics, and triggers.
3. Execute and ensure adoption happens.

Our toolbox can help equip you to successfully sail through all of them. Here's how the tools will help you navigate adoption.

MOMENTS OF TRUTH

Determine your moments of truth during the adoption process (you likely did this while building your customer journey map and/or Customer Success Plan), so you can execute, demonstrate, and deliver on them. Map out all the moments of truth during the adoption process and think about how you can improve them to make the customer's experience better and more valuable.

PLAYBOOKS

Playbooks help the CSM know what to do when specific scenarios occur. They are full of examples, case studies, and templates to help the CSM manage the scenarios successfully. You may have playbooks to refer to from other customers or find you need to create them when new situations occur.

You should build a playbook for these three main scenarios and deploy each during the adoption phase:

- **The customer has no usage.** The product has been deployed, but none of the customer's employees are using it yet.
- **The customer has low usage.** Initially, everyone was using the product, but after three months, half the users dropped off.
- **The customer isn't getting business value.** They aren't operationally dependent.

Create a playbook for each of these scenarios, but remember, playbooks aren't meant to be perfect—they're meant to be iterated and fine-tuned. When building out the playbooks, focus on the usability of the playbook and get feedback from your team.

CUSTOMER HEALTH

When we discussed onboarding in the last chapter, I mentioned six different areas we typically consider when determining customer health. Here they are again as a reminder:

- **Product usage:** Does your customer have operational dependence on the product (is your customer using the product)?
- **Business outcomes:** Is your customer seeing value and realizing their desired business outcomes?
- **Customer sentiment:** Are we looking at customer feedback and acting on it (voice of the customer)?
- **Relationship strength:** Have we identified an executive sponsor? Do we have ambassadors/champions/power users identified? How many references have they provided? What rate of surveys are completed? Have they contributed to online blogs or spoken at your company's annual conferences?
- **Services optimization:** Is the customer using all the capabilities

of your company (services, training, customer community, events, premium offerings)?

- **Support and operations:** Are we delivering a good customer experience at the many touch points in the process (customer support, accurate invoicing)?

Which of these questions are important during adoption?

At this stage in the journey (adoption), some questions will be more important than others. For example, during adoption, the customer probably isn't operationally dependent on the solution or tapping into all your company's capabilities outright. So we know those questions aren't as important as, say, "Are we delivering a good customer experience thus far (from sales handover to provisioning of licenses, to onboarding, training, etc.)?" You will need to determine which questions are vital and statistically weigh them accordingly based on voice of the customer, CSM input, and overall feedback from both your company and your customer.

CUSTOMER RISK

We know there are eight different types of customer risk, but during the adoption phase, it's essential to focus on relationship risk, the loss of key champions and sponsors. There is acute relationship risk and persistent relationship risk.

- **Acute relationship risk:** Acute relationship risk happens quickly—for example, when the customer goes out of business (which is completely out of your control). Acute relationship risk also happens when your key champion or program sponsor leaves the organization unexpectedly. "I quit yesterday and I'm leaving tomorrow." If this happens to you, you need to be proactive and ask, "Who is the incumbent? How do I get introduced? Are there any connections between that person and an executive from my company?" You can't just wait and see what happens. You need to be proactive about gaining the confidence of your sponsor's replacement. Start winning them over on day one (or prior through broadening the relationships in the account).

- **Persistent relationship risk:** Persistent relationship risk happens slowly over time. It's little problems, such as bugs and disorganized resource sites, that wear your customer down because every experience gets worse. This can be very irritating for the customer, so they bail out and stop using your product by finding something easier to use (a better experience). Persistent relationship risk also occurs when we as customer success leaders fail to nurture new company champions. Every time we do, we're losing out on someone who could have been a product evangelist and who could have been teaching others how to use it. Fostering new key champions is just as crucial as nurturing existing ones.

CUSTOMER SUCCESS PLAN

Each customer success plan should have a section on adoption. Make sure you know who the stakeholders are and have a timeline of key events and triggers. Will there be training tutorials and/or key events? Capture it in the Customer Success Plan.

The Customer Success Plan for adoption should also include milestones, metrics, KPIs, customer health, and a list of all the different types of people who need to use your product or service.

SEGMENTATION

For adoption, segmentation is used to determine training time and the methodology needed to gain operational dependence and deliver value for the customer as quickly as possible.

First, a customer's time is valuable and limited. Demonstrate an understanding of this by personalizing their product training experience—for example, narrowing down a week-long training program to half a day would be extremely valuable, or a half-day training program into one hour (specific to the pieces that are needed at that time for the customer). A five-day training program is hard to stomach. Wouldn't it be better to instead tailor the training to your customer and save them time?

Segmentation will also help you determine *how* you're going to deliver the training. Will it be high touch with a personalized program? Or will e-learning suffice? A combination perhaps? Segmentation will help you determine the specifics you need to deliver a successful training program.

TIPS AND TRICKS FOR ADOPTION

If there is one thing to take away from this chapter about adoption, it's to go and find your company champions. They will help with the adoption process; they will be your evangelist for change management, training, and operational dependence.

When my boss handed me my first iPhone way back when, he didn't evangelize it. He didn't train me, and he didn't tell me how consumers (like me) were benefiting from it. He didn't say:

"Check out this new phone, Wayne! It's going to change the future of mobile devices. I've been using mine for only a week and I'm already hooked. I know you like your BlackBerry, but if you give the iPhone a try, you're going to love it. Personally, I'm seeing tremendous value. Do you want me to quickly show you a few basics so you know how to navigate it?"

Back then, my boss wasn't an iPhone champion. He was just a guy who thought it would make a good gift. If he *had* been, I probably would have given the iPhone a try when I first received it. I probably wouldn't have given it to my executive business partner. Succeeding in adoption means finding your company champions.

It also means using the tools you have at your disposal. Identify those moments of truth, write those Customer Success Plans, and calculate those customer health scores. You can even go so far as to create a playbook for your customer to use themselves. (Yes, the same tool we rely on to deliver best practices at scale can be used here for your customers.) Customers don't know the best practices and potential traps because they've never rolled out your software before. If you give them an adoption playbook, you're providing them with an asset that adds value and removes risk, and your stakeholder will love you for it.

Hold formal and informal training events to help drive successful adoption (the office hours I mentioned earlier in the chapter are a great example of an informal training event) and reward your customer's employees who are rolling out adoption effectively and who are operationally dependent. Turn them into champions.

You know you're successful when the sales team invites you to meetings with their prospects to demonstrate your process (such as how you will help make the implementation a success). That's how you know you've nailed adoption (and onboarding).

But customer success doesn't end there (I think you probably know that). Now that the customer has adopted your product, it's time to get them to renew. Pillar #4: Retention is coming up next.

CHAPTER 6

PILLAR #4: RETENTION

"VALUED SUSTAINED"

The Seven Customer Success Pillars

Customer Journey Lifecycle Stages

Operationalize CS · Onboarding · Adoption · Retention · Expansion · Advocacy · Strategic Advisor

www.cspillars.com

Bain & Company, a management consulting firm headquartered in Boston, conducted a study that concluded a 5% increase in customer retention leads to a 25% increase in profits.[6] Think about that for a second: a small increase in retention leads to massive profits for your company—each retained customer is very profitable. Those numbers matter to your board of directors. The study demonstrates the high cost of landing a new customer. Retaining existing customers costs a lot less.

"If a typical SaaS business loses about 2% to 3% of their customers each month to churn, the business must grow by at least 27% to 43% annually to maintain the same revenue."

—TOMASZ TUNGUZ[7]

If you need any proof to convince your board that it's the right strategy, Tomasz just handed it to you (mic drop).

Retaining customers and eliminating churn is a CSM's number one responsibility. It is probably more pivotal than driving increased value, improving the customer experience (and satisfaction), and facilitating customer acquisition through advocacy, although one could argue that those activities are integrated into retention (yes, let's start the debate). Customer retention is the one metric we have that solidifies whether we're doing a good job.

WHAT IS CUSTOMER RETENTION?

The future success of every organization depends on retaining present customers. In this chapter, we're going to discuss retention, which means focusing on ensuring the customer gets and

---

6   Fred Reichheld, "Prescription for Cutting Costs," Bain & Company, accessed January 14, 2021, https://media.bain.com/Images/BB_Prescription_cutting_costs.pdf.

7   Tomasz Tunguz, "Why Customer Success Is an Essential Part of Every SaaS Startup," blog on tomtunguz.com, October 11, 2013, https://tomtunguz.com/churn/.

renews. Onboarding was excellent, adoption ran smoothly, but now what? How do we sustain value in the account and build a relationship with our customer that gets them to stay?

First, let's define customer retention so we're all on the same page.

> Customer retention is the carefully orchestrated process whereby the customer chooses to extend their relationship with you.

If we break that sentence down, *carefully orchestrated process* means we're increasing the odds of the customer renewing because we've deployed a number of strategies, activities, and playbooks to achieve outcomes that lend themselves to creating an environment that entices the customer to stay.

The customer chooses simply means the customer is in control. Retention is a customer-driven event. When most of us think "retention," we think we have to do something, but retention means the customer is making a choice on whether to stay with your company. We can pull a few levers during the renewal conversation, but at the end of the day, the customer has to choose to stay. So we want to make the retention process, and everything leading up to it, a positive experience.

The last part of the definition, *to extend their relationship with you*, represents a key point. The number one reason a customer leaves is because they aren't seeing value. But what if you've done a good job? If you've provided value in the past, the customer should automatically renew, right?

Not so fast! The customer doesn't choose to stay with you

because of the historical value you've driven for them—they stay because of the vision and promise of the future you have painted with them.

> They trust you because you have driven value in the past, but they will continue to work with you because of the *future* value you promise to provide.

This is a subtle but powerful difference. Customers are thinking about the future, so you can't simply look at the past to forecast customer retention. It's heartbreaking, but a value-driven past doesn't guarantee a rosy future.

When you say, "We drove so much value for you! Why are you leaving?"

Your customer says, "We found another vendor that had a better vision and a more innovative approach."

If the customer chooses not to renew—despite the good service you've provided—it's because of the future, not the past. If you do a good job, it doesn't mean they'll stay, so don't get lulled in by a false sense of security. To retain your customers, you have to prove you will provide them with value in the future.

THE DEADLIEST WORD IN THE SAAS STRATOSPHERE— CHURN

Do you know what happens when you don't retain a customer?

If you answered, "You lose revenue," you are 100% correct!

But reduced revenue isn't the only negative aspect of losing a customer. In fact, there are another half a dozen negatives that come from customer churn.

1. Every time a customer churns, you miss out on a lot more. You've lost your ability to upsell that customer on new products, features, and solutions. That's future revenue you'll no longer be able to tap into.

2. Also, every customer comes with behavioral data you can analyze and glean for insights. When you lose one, you lose access to data points and consumption habits that can help you make better product and marketing decisions. When the customer doesn't renew, you lose the ability to glean insights from their interaction with your product and/or service.

3. Future ideas such as "It would be great if you did this!" or "If you did that, it would be a game changer!" are pieces of gold from your customers. One of these ideas could become your product's "sticky feature" and your competitive differentiator. Every time you lose a customer, you're losing someone who might have an idea that transforms your product.

4. Not to mention, losing customers helps your competition. When your customers leave you to go to a competitor, the competitor now has access to your former customer's intellectual property and insight into their industry, vertical, and business. They're also getting customer feedback, feature requests (what if their request is the one that revolutionizes the industry?), and the potential for customer advocacy. All this strengthens your competition.

5. Losing a customer impacts the internal team, too. Your entire company is negatively affected when customers don't renew because it's distracting to the organization. If a big customer decides not to renew, executives start to freak out: they jump on plans, offer massive discounts, and scramble to

put together a "get well" plan or a customer success "SWAT team." But when the focus is on immediate fixes, it means these executives (and everyone else involved) are putting out fires rather than focusing on long-term retention strategies, which only causes more of these problems in the future.

Finally, when a customer doesn't renew, the CSM feels the pain, maybe more than anyone.

Picture this...

6. You are the CSM for a big, global customer. Every day, you wake up, grab your coffee, check your email, and make sure your customer is seeing value from your company's solution. You travel, visit global offices, meet people, and build relationships, but suddenly, after three years of service, the customer decides not to renew their contract with you. You've provided value in the past, but they decide to leave anyway. And when they do, it feels almost like breakup. You feel demoralized and dejected.

What did I do wrong? Will my other customers leave, too? Will I get to keep my job?

The more customers you lose, the more you're chipping away at the health of your customer success manager team, which can lead to other issues such as reduced employee engagement or even attrition. Lost revenue remains the most significant loss, but studies show these other losses impact the bottom line as well.

NO ~~SOUP~~ RENEWAL FOR YOU!

Retention is an ongoing set of activities and strategies in many moments of truth throughout the customer journey and life cycle. The renewal is a single event, a milestone that signals your retention strategies worked.

The number one reason a customer doesn't renew is because they don't achieve the business value that was promised or desired. No value equals no renewal. So, above all else, we need to make sure the customer always sees value.

When you develop the customer Customer Success Plan, you talk about the customer's desired outcome from using your solution. You determine the value they seek.

You don't need to be the star of your own Sherlock Holmes detective novel, scouring London to find clues that will help you figure out the customer's desired outcome. All you have to do is ask—and listen to their answers.

It gets tricky once you've solved the first problem, though. You may have to work hard to find opportunities within the customer's organization. Your stakeholder may not have any additional problems to solve, but other potential stakeholders at their organization might.

How do you get an introduction to that stakeholder? How do you navigate inside an organization to determine its pain points?

There are easy, nonstressful solutions to this problem. You can read your customer's annual report. You can also actively listen to conversations at your QBRs (I described QBRs in Chapter 2, if you need a refresher) and in the regular meetings you have with your customer (you should be doing all that anyway) so you can pick up on other areas where you can provide value. You can proactively ask to be introduced to employee champions inside your customer base, too, to brainstorm and discover new pain points. If you can identify a problem the customer didn't know they needed solved, you've provided future value.

RENEWAL RATE, GROSS RETENTION, AND NET RETENTION, OH MY

The renewal is fundamental in the retention process, and the renewal rate is key when determining gross retention and net retention. It's a number you give to your board of directors and a number you potentially base compensation on. There are four reasons why every organization should care about measuring their renewal rate:

1. **We can trend data over time and see whether we're doing a good job.** It tells us if we're getting better or worse. It is a lagging indicator, but it's an indicator nonetheless, and we should take note of it continuously.
2. **It allows us to be more proactive.** It can give us insights as to what's going wrong (and what's going right) so we can move the project forward as quickly and effectively as possible.
3. **It indicates a healthy, profitable business.** If you have strong retention, it indicates your company is currently profitable or will be profitable in the future. Retaining customers increases your future growth opportunity by maximizing your customers' lifetime value.
4. **It serves as an early warning system.** Maybe your largest customers are renewing easily, but your mid-market space has challenges and problems. If you have a strong or healthy

renewal business, a dip in this rate can signal if something is potentially wrong.

HOW DO WE MEASURE THE RENEWAL RATE?

Gross revenue retention (GRR) looks at how much of the customer base you've kept year over year without including expansion revenue. The easy way to calculate this is:

(current ARR – reductions – churn) / starting ARR

And due to this formula, the number will always be 100% or less.

Net revenue retention (NRR) is similar to GRR, except you add any expansion (upsells, cross-sells, price increases). The formula looks like this:

(ARR + expansion – reductions – churn) / starting ARR

A healthy SaaS business has net dollar retention of over 100%, because expansion in the customer base is outpacing reductions and churn.

FORECASTING RETENTION AND YOU

An effective customer success organization forecasts retention more accurately by tracking renewal rates. That's why we operationalize customer success. All the tools we have at our disposal—Customer Success Plans, health scores, and so forth—are meant to help us have better future predictability so the company can allocate dollars more efficiently.

In other words, if you're consistently hitting your renewals forecasts, finance is comfortable spending money as planned. This could mean more investment in data analytics, personnel, and software platforms to run your business. Whatever those investments are, when the renewal rate is as predicted, finance feels comfortable.

On the other hand, if you have a ton of surprises (such as a customer decides not to renew and you had no clue), finance will get a little skittish. They will assume other surprises are coming. If the surprises are big enough, finance may put you on a hiring freeze and suspend your expense budgets, which only further disrupts your business. Do you think this activity leads to more churn? Absolutely it does! Accurate retention forecasting is paramount for every customer success organization.

CSMS AND RETENTION SITTIN' IN A TREE

The renewal process can be managed by sales, account managers, CSMs, or if the company is big enough, a renewals team (that may even sit within the customer success team. More on all of that later), but a CSM knows their customer inside and out. They understand their pain points and best know how to solve their problems. It makes sense they influence the renewal process, right? I have seen three different ways CSMs have influenced the process.

1. GUIDE THE PROCESS

I've seen CSMs guide the process of renewals directly in collaboration with the renewal manager for that account. In most cases, the CSM is the expert on the problems the customer wants to solve and the solution that works. By working hand in hand with the renewal manager, a better forecast can be created (by communicating Customer Success Plan progress and QBR/EBR feedback, etc.), potential issues can be nipped in the bud before renewal time, and better insights for potential expansion can be identified early.

2. TRANSACTIONAL INCREASES

There are also examples in the industry of CSMs handling transactional increases. In other words, if a customer uses 75 licenses but their contract allows for 50, they will initiate the conversation to update the contract to include the additional 25 licenses. Typically, these conversations are initiated with the CSMs, so it's reasonable for them to handle the transaction. Typically, I see this in smaller organizations (less than $50 million in ARR) where the CSM has more hats than at larger organizations.

3. MANAGE THE RENEWAL

Finally, I have seen CSMs manage the entire renewal process. In addition to their regular responsibilities (such as understanding and driving value, creating operational dependence, nurturing and finding advocates, etc.), they are also responsible for the renewal transaction with the customer. This means upselling, cross-selling, changes to SLAs, and any commercial agreement changes, typically in companies with less than $20 million in ARR.

NOW IT'S TIME TO CREATE A RENEWALS TEAM

Once you approach $100 million in ARR, I highly recommend creating a dedicated renewals team whose sole job is to manage contract renewals. At that point, you have enough revenue to justify role specialization.

The number of uses will differ depending on whether you're a B2C or B2B company, a digital native company, or traditional business. But as a general rule of thumb, $100 million signifies when it's time to mature your customer success function and create a specialized renewal team. And due to the interconnectivity of both the CSM and renewal manager role, I recommend these two functions live under the same leader (head of customer success or chief customer officer).

HOW CAN OUR TOOLBOX HELP?

How do we leverage the tools in our toolbox to assist with renewals? We first start with moments of truth.

MOMENTS OF TRUTH

Many of the customer's moments of truth live in the onboarding and adoption phases. By the time we get to the renewal, we need to make sure we can prove value, so we need to list out all the moments of truth ahead of time and make sure we execute them exceptionally. This may mean working with other departments within your organization to help them make their processes more customer success friendly.

We have to be conscious of delivering value through moments of truth through the renewal and beyond, and we need to make sure the stakeholder recognizes this value. Do they agree that you provided value? Is it defensible? Is it measurable and real? Is it causation as opposed to correlation? Can you apply business value consulting techniques to measure impact?

Provide your customer with proof that you have provided value so they can present it to their leadership. This is how you use moments of truth to get the renewal.

PLAYBOOKS

There are two retention playbooks I think every customer success organization should have: one for renewals and one for identifying renewal risks.

RENEWAL PLAYBOOK

The renewal playbook illustrates the process of renewing a customer and the tasks and efforts that get the customer to sign on the dotted line. When creating it, you should first have an internal review with everyone who is vested in the customer's renewal.

The appropriate timeline will vary company to company and industry to industry (as it should). I can't give you an exact time frame of when to get started, but I can give you the steps to work backward and figure it out yourself. Working backward allows you to set a more realistic timeline for when the playbook should begin execution.

If the last step in the process is signing the agreement, what comes right before that? Does the customer's legal team need to review and approve before the stakeholder can sign? How about a step before that? In order for the contract to be renewed, it has to be prepared (I don't recommend repurposing contracts ever). How long does that take? Go back another step, and we'll see that in order to draft a new contract, we have to have a conversation with the customer. But we can't have that conversation until we've given the customer their renewal notice. How much time will that step take?

Each step takes a certain number of days, and when you add it all up, you know approximately when to get the renewal process started. Work backward until you get to the internal review, and you will have created your renewals playbook timeline and steps. And to briefly remind you, the format is irrelevant as long as it gets the job done.

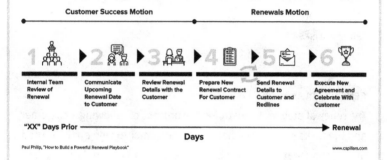

Sample Renewal Playbook Timeline

Paul Philip, "How to Build a Powerful Renewal Playbook"   www.cspillars.com

CUSTOMER HEALTH

Leading up to the renewal, one of the fundamental questions we should ask ourselves is, *what is the customer health score?*

As we've talked about, customer health can be centrally developed by a data science and analytics team, or it can be calculated by the CSM using the six questions presented earlier. Remember to weigh the metrics to account for different phases in the customer life cycle (we talked about this, too).

You need to measure customer health leading up to the renewal. If it's unhealthy, it doesn't look good for the renewal, so we need to make sure we're laser-focused on it throughout the retention phase. We also want to see how it's trending. Are we seeing improvements and gaining momentum? If we are, we can leverage that during the renewals process. "We started off on the wrong foot, but we're getting better. We made some adjustments and now we've really hit our stride. We're going to get better to help you get better."

Understanding your customer health score and how it's trending will help you understand and drive the narrative of the renewal conversation you're going to have with your customer.

CUSTOMER RISK

Of the eight types of customer risk, product fit risk really begins to emerge during the Retention Pillar. This risk looks at nonstandard use cases such as the customer isn't ready for your product yet, or your product wasn't able to deliver the desired or promised value.

Product fit risk appears acutely, but the symptoms are persistent. Typically, this occurs when the customer isn't using the product as intended, or they're not ready to commit yet because they are waiting to take full advantage of the product. The second circumstance is much less obvious.

Regardless, they aren't seeing value, so they get frustrated and more and more irritated over time until they eventually decide to leave.

The problem is persistent, which is why you have to look out for complaints as early as the initial deployment or leverage the data team's customer health scores. But without hovering over the users and watching how they use the product, it's hard to see. That's why I suggest doing a ride-along. Product fit risk is more subtle than the other risks and takes extra effort to curb.

CUSTOMER SUCCESS PLANS

If you think about it, Customer Success Plans have been around for a long time. I can just picture a caveman drawing a Customer Success Plan on the wall of a cave.

1. Find animal.
2. Kill animal.
3. Eat animal.

In the SaaS and cloud worlds, Customer Success Plans aren't that simple (or violent), and the desired outcome isn't the same. But ultimately, the concepts *are*—find a way to share a best practice with others so they can learn how to improve. We just happen to call it something different.

The ultimate outcome of a Customer Success Plan is the renewal. Longer term expansion could be the primary focus, but until we retain the customer, we shouldn't think about expansion.

When it comes to the renewal, there are three questions you have to answer.

1. ARE WE ON TRACK TO ACHIEVING OUR DEFINED GOALS?

You've defined your customer's value one (and value two, three, four, and five) and their desired outcomes. Now you want to track them to see if you're on target to provide the value you promised. If you're clear on what these values and outcomes are and can prove the value you provided, you should.

Remind the customer, "Remember when you said you would really love it if you could solve this problem and we did?"

If you're clear on the customer's goals, you can clearly demonstrate the value you provided.

2. WHAT DOES CONSUMPTION LOOK LIKE?

This doesn't apply only to licenses. It could be the number of service hours your company promised the customer, or compute power provisioned, or the amount of bandwidth you're providing.

The point is, what does the customer's consumption look like? If they bought 1,000 licenses but are using only 100, do you think the chances are high they'll renew? And if they do renew, how many licenses do you think they'll want?

Leading up to the renewal, we need to make sure we're aware of our customer's product consumption and get them as close to that number as possible.

3. HAVE THEY ADOPTED THE STICKY FEATURES OF OUR PRODUCT?

As mentioned earlier, I was talking to a peer of mine at an identity management company, and they told me they used to have a complex customer health scoring system. However, when the data scientists did the analysis, they found the biggest predictor of churn was whether the customer had deployed three main features or not. Very quickly, they eliminated a lot of risk management inefficiencies—everyone, from services to support to customer success, can align on getting usage of those features.

SEGMENTATION

Segmentation should be heavily used in the Retention Pillar because you don't want to miss easy opportunities.

Let me explain.

Segmentation will give you an idea of how easy or hard the renewal will be. Multiyear contracts, for example, need less focus and are better for your company because everyone's job is easier. It's easier for the renewals team, more consistent outcomes for the finance team, and reducing the workload on the legal team. You create efficiencies and better predictability by securing multiyear renewals.

You should also segment renewals based on risk. Identify your riskiest accounts and start working on their renewal sooner. Accounts that are safe, trending well, and in good health can wait a little longer. Of course, your playbook will help you plan when to begin the renewal process.

Mostly, you are segmenting your time (and your priorities) in the Retention Pillar. I have seen some CSMs manage 250 accounts, which is nuts! But when you segment your time properly, it's easier to scale.

CUSTOMER DELIGHT

Not always obvious, but the renewals process doesn't have to be just a transaction—it can be an event that celebrates the renewal of a partnership of success. Recently, I received renewal notices from several companies that were "delightful" to receive. They stated they hate corporate notices and wanted to let me know they loved our partnership. Animated GIFs were included when the renewal manager celebrated an upcoming renewal. The wording was light and fun and, when compared to other vendors, created a differentiated experience. Of course, we would need to be selective on whom to send this type of communication to (Hint: healthy, happy customers).

TIPS AND TRICKS FOR RETENTION

If it's low risk and low value, put this account on maintenance mode.

If it's high risk and high value, or low risk and high value, put in time and effort.

If it's high risk and low value, transition to retention mode.

This will help determine where CSMs spend time and how to focus the team.

BE THE GROWTH ENGINE YOU WERE BORN TO BE

Customer retention means being continuously focused on the customers' desired outcomes. It means understanding your customers thoroughly, more than just their goals and desired outcomes. You need to know their *personalities*. Is the stakeholder driven by ego? Are they altruistic? Recognizing these nuances will change the way you approach an account. It will change the words you use and even the playbooks you write. Remember, a customer's goals and objectives are always changing. The value of a CSM is their ability to adjust.

The customer success organization is a growth engine for your company. Many people still think of it solely as a retention team, but as we've talked about, that's an old-school way of thinking. Today's most successful businesses are also focused on growth. In the next chapter, we're going to talk about expansion.

CHAPTER 7

PILLAR #5: EXPANSION

"VALUE EXPANDED"

The Seven Customer Success Pillars

Customer Journey Lifecycle Stages

Operationalize CS · Onboarding · Adoption · Retention · Expansion · Advocacy · Strategic Advisor

www.cspillars.com

In 2011 in Woodlands, Texas, I completed my first Ironman.

I was battered, bruised, and I had a stress fracture, but I was so happy, so *amazed* by my accomplishment, I wanted to do it again. And I wanted to do it *better*.

Despite my complete and utter exhaustion and the pain I literally felt over my entire body (I think my organs throbbed, too), I said:

"I want more of this! It feels good!"

It was crazy, but I was hooked. Finishing an Ironman is a feeling like no other. I have since done two more for a total of three. My second race was in Coeur d'Alene, Idaho, and my third (with a time that was three hours better than my first time in Texas, thank you very much) was in Tempe, Arizona.

WHAT IS EXPANSION?

Customer expansion—the goal of pretty much every corporation everywhere (even Ironman). But what is it? And why is it so indispensable?

In my opinion, it all boils down to one sentence:

> *Customer expansion occurs when a customer finds value in your solution and grants you the opportunity to increase that value.*

When we break that sentence down, the first phrase encapsulates the main idea I've expressed throughout this book: *a customer finds value in your solution.* The ultimate goal of a CSM is to drive value for the customer and ensure they get to their desired outcome and the most out of their investment. Customer expansion cannot happen until a customer sees value.

The next piece of the definition—*grant you*—indicates the customer is in the driver's seat. (I can think of a handful of examples where a customer is contractually obligated to expand their business with you, but we're not here to talk about that.) Customer success wants expansion to happen because the customer is so satisfied by the value you're driving that they're interested in engaging in a deeper relationship. The customer *grants* you the opportunity to work with them again.

Finally, the *opportunity to increase value* simply refers to selling additional products, services, and solutions, the so-called upsell or cross-sell.

THE MANY FACES OF EXPANSION

When I ask for examples of customer expansion, I typically hear two common types—upselling and cross-selling. We'll focus on those in the Expansion Pillar, but there are other types of expansion activities we don't want to forget about.

For example, when a customer is trialing your software and then becomes a paid customer (from a freemium or paid proof-of-concept model), that's expansion. At least, I see it that way because the financial relationship expands. Sales typically runs this type of expansion.

The renewals team also has expansion opportunities—they can increase prices. Most successful subscription companies either build in contractual price increases or negotiate them at the end of the contract. Most customers who see value won't balk at a 3% to 5% increase because we've done a good job convincing them of future value—that is, the product is getting better, there will be more features, you'll see even more value.

There are also multiyear conversions that count as an example of expansion. What do I mean by that? Let's say a customer is on a one- to three-year contract and it's time to renew. If you can convince the customer to change to a three- to *five*-year contract, you've completed a multiyear conversion. You have expanded the contractual obligation and thus expanded contractual revenue in the future.

It's good to know the different expansion types that exist, but as mentioned earlier, this chapter is about the two most common—upselling and cross-selling.

UPSELLING

Upselling is buying more of the same thing you already have. It's supersizing your meal so you get a bigger portion of food. The most obvious example of this is supersizing your McDonald's fries, and upgrading from a medium to a large. Upselling is selling more of the same.

Are you wondering, *why is upselling an essential part of expansion?* The way I see it, there are three main reasons.

1. Combat the High Cost of Acquiring New Logos

The first is that it helps you combat the high cost of acquiring new logos. ProfitWell is a subscription software that helps their customers increase recurring revenue growth faster. They reported on a 2016 Pacific Crest survey that shows the *median* cost of acquisition of one new dollar of revenue for a new logo was $1.16.[8] The medium cost for renewing a customer (of one

---

8   Patrick Campbell, "Expansion Revenue: How Much Do You Need to Be Successful?" Profitwell.com, November 9, 2018, https://www.profitwell.com/recur/all/how-much-expansion-revenue-to-be-successful.

dollar) is $0.13,[9] which further proves what we already know—acquiring a new customer is more expensive than retaining an existing one, in this case by $0.18.

But what is the cost of *upselling* a customer? The same Pacific Crest study found the medium cost of upselling a customer is $0.27 and $0.20 for expansions.[10] This will differ from company to company. It could be as high as $0.55 or as low as $0.10. Regardless, in every case, the data tells us it's more profitable to upsell a customer than acquire a new one. If all we did was sell new customers, we'd likely lose a ton of money and eventually go out of business. Upselling allows you to offset the cost of new customer acquisition.

2. Mitigate Churn

Second, it's also an easy way to mitigate churn. If a customer wants to buy more of what they have, it's a good sign they're going to stay.

3. Identify the Right Customers

Last, it helps you identify the right customers. When you're a new software company, it's hard to know who the best customers are right off the bat. If a customer is granting you the opportunity to add more value, that's a good sign this customer is one of your best.

---

9   David Skok, "2016 Pacific Crest SaaS Survey—Part 1," ForEntrepreneurs.com, accessed January 14, 2021, http://www.forentrepreneurs.com/2016-saas-survey-part-1/.

10 Campbell, "Expansion Revenue."

CROSS-SELLING

Cross-selling happens when you offer your customer *other* products and services. If they already have a large order of fries, cross-selling means selling them a hamburger, a soda, and a piece of warm apple pie.

A customer initially buys your solution because they have an issue or a challenge they're trying to solve. They come to you for one thing and may not be familiar with the other offerings you have. You might have software products and services that would help solve your customer's additional problems.

It is crucial your customer success organization (and specifically your CSM) *understands* as many (if not all) the products and services the company provides because ultimately, they're trying to look for additional areas where they can help drive value and solve the customer's problems, but cross-selling doesn't typically fall in the list of CSM responsibilities.

You want sales to focus on selling so your CSM can focus on the customer and find additional challenges and inefficiencies to add value and consumption. When the CSM is free to concentrate on the customer and their Customer Success Plan, they'll be able to identify the hurdles that trip them up constantly and actively look for solutions.

I once was on the client side and worked with a CSM who was so invested in my business (and understood my challenges and industry so well) they were able to point to other products and services in the market that existed to help me. These weren't products their company offered, just products the CSM knew I needed. That CSM was the greatest CSM in the whole world to me.

Cross-selling is about expanding the customer's understanding of your company to help them achieve better value and better outcomes.

WHAT IS UPTELLING?

In 2019, I advised a global company that was building a CSM organization with people in over 60 countries. As part of that exercise, I got to work with a leader named Zinnia. I don't know if she invented the term *uptell*, but she was certainly the one who introduced me to it. She told me, "CSMs don't upsell or cross-sell; they uptell."

In other words, they educate the customer. They make the customer aware of capabilities that may help solve problems. CSMs tell the customer about related solutions and use cases that may drive value and solve their current challenges. They uptell.

I think that word is so spot-on that I use it all the time now.

EXPANSION: THE VITAL FRONTIER

Are you asking yourself, *why is expansion revenue so vital?*

By now you know, from a cost perspective, it's much cheaper to expand revenue than generate it. But consider an even more significant mathematical reason why expansion is preeminent to the success of every business. As your company grows, if you have a constant churn rate within your customer base, the amount of churn will increase at a *significantly* faster rate than your company's ability to acquire new revenue.

For example, if I churn 10% of $1 million in revenue, I've

churned $100,000. In order for me to make up that revenue, I have to sell $100,000 worth of new business just to get back to the original starting point. However, if I'm at $1 billion in revenue and I churn 10%, I've lost $100 million in revenue. That's a much harder number to make up. Just think of the number of transactions, customers, and activities needed to make up for that churned revenue. And that only gets you back to square one. In order to grow, you'll have to do even more.

Churn gets larger over time, whereas new customer acquisition is more linear. There exists only a certain number of $100,000 customers out there, and if I have to make up for $100 million in churn, I'm going to need a thousand of them. The point I'm trying to make here is that once your company scales, it becomes impossible to offset your churn purely by adding new customers to your customer base.

So what do we do? How do we make up for churned revenue as our company grows and scales?

The only real solution is to generate more wallet share from your existing customers. You have to prove you've driven to value in the past and convince them you will continue to drive value in the future. You have to uptell, then you upsell and cross-sell about "what's possible."

A BIGGER IMPACT ON EXPANSION

ProfitWell conducted another study worth mentioning. They looked at data from about 2,000 companies and found that for businesses without a customer success function, the median percentage of revenue generated from customer expansion was less than 10%. For companies *with* a customer success function, that median percentage increased to 22%. In the 75th percentile, the percentage of revenue generated from expansion was as high as 35%.[11]

Patrick Campbell, the CEO of ProfitWell, expanded on the study and how it relates to gross retention rate (GRR). If I have a 10% churn problem and am only renewing 90% of my revenue each year, the best I can do is improve by 10% and take my current GRR of 90% up to 100%. "We've retained 100% of last year's customer revenue." My impact is limited by whatever percentage gap exists between retention and churn. In this case, it's 10%.[12]

When we think about expansion, however, if I can increase a customer's wallet spend from $100,000 to $5 million—a 50x or 5,000% increase—it's much more impactful than a 10% GRR increase. Campbell points out the data shows customer success is much more impactful when focusing on expansion versus retention.[13]

This is an evolution in the customer success life cycle. If you recall, customer success used to solely focus on retention and making the customer happy at all costs—"Deliver value, secure the renewal, get as high a retention rate as possible"—but we've realized that that was like sitting at the kids' table at Thanksgiving. Customer success deserves a spot at the grown-up table because expansion is significantly more impactful to the overall success of the organization.

---

11 Patrick Campbell, "Customer Success Reduces Churn and Increases Expansion Revenue," ProfitWell.com, October 10, 2018, https://www.profitwell.com/recur/all/customer-success-impacts-retention-and-churn.

12 Patrick Campbell, "How to Calculate Churn Rate: 4 Formulas for Calculating Churn," ProfitWell.com, May 27, 2020, https://www.profitwell.com/customer-churn/calculate-churn-rate.

13 Campbell, "Customer Success Reduces Churn."

Even though CSMs aren't really responsible for sales, the evidence and the data support the idea that customer success has an even bigger impact on expansion (or consumption in an IaaS, infrastructure as a service, environment) than they do on retention. That's why it's massively substantial that we as customer success leaders nail this pillar.

THE CSM AND EXPANSION DO-SI-DO

We've talked a lot about how powerful customer success is to customer expansion, but we've also established that CSMs aren't responsible for sales. So what is a CSM's role in expansion? What is their function?

From my perspective, a CSM can impact expansion in two different ways. The first is passive expansion. If you've successfully moved through pillars 1 through 4—onboarding, adoption, and retention—you've already created an opportunity for the customer to expand their business with you. You created operational dependence, you've driven to value, and you've maxed out your customer's license consumption. You've created an environment where the customer will buy more licenses as the company grows. You have impacted expansion.

The second way a CSM can impact expansion is through active expansion via something called a customer success qualified lead, otherwise known as a CSQL.

MARKETING QUALIFIED LEADS

Before we delve in deeper to CSQLs, we first need to understand marketing qualified leads (MQLs). An MQL is a lead that marketing funnels to the sales team to close. This is the presale period, which some argue is an *additional* pillar. (I'm not quite sold on the whole pillar #1.5 idea, but the idea is popular enough that I've carved out some space for it at the end of this book.)

How does marketing find *qualified* leads? First, they target customers in specific industries and verticals (they sometimes target use cases and specific brands as well). They target these customers through advertising, tailored website copy, and drip email campaigns. If someone visits the website and downloads a white paper, that's an opportunity for marketing to pursue. Marketing also targets customers at trade shows, conferences, and given our pandemic life, webinars.

Once marketing has targeted leads, those leads need to be converted to *qualified* leads. Typically, this means inputting leads into the company's CRM tool. Sales then reviews the leads and pursues any they believe they can close. Creating MQLs is a routine marketing function.

CUSTOMER SUCCESS QUALIFIED LEADS

In the world of customer success, CSMs target customers and turn them into qualified leads. If you're a CSM, look at your existing customer base for opportunities to increase value by either upselling, cross-selling, or both. You then input the details of those opportunities into your CRM for sales to review and pursue.

The rest of the process is the same for CSQLs as it is for MQLs. Sales takes the lead and reaches out to the customer to start a conversation (but with a huge amount of information about the customer and desired outcomes). Once they realize the CSQL is sound, they put effort into creating the proposal and closing the deal.

What's really exciting about CSQLs are the results. MQLs convert anywhere between 5% and 20%. There is less data available for CSQLs (they haven't been around as long), but from what I have experienced, CSQLs convert between 60% and 70%.

This makes sense because as a CSM, you know more about your customer than marketing does. You're also working with a much smaller pool of prospects who are already engaged. Marketing has the hard job of trying to navigate the old structure and determine who the stakeholders are and who owns the budget. If you're the CSM, you already know all those details—they're written down in your Customer Success Plan. You know the people, you know the politics, and you know the timing. You know so much more because you're on the inside.

HOW TO IMPLEMENT CSQLS

When it comes to qualified leads, a CSM has it much easier than a marketing manager, and as a result, their leads are stronger. You as a CSM have access to more customer data than marketing does, making your CSQLs a pivotal component of the sales cycle. As mentioned, you capture the data and pass it on to sales. Let's look at that process in more detail.

First, you have to capture the CSQL. Once you determine if the customer has a clear, qualified need (which can be done by uncovering an inefficiency inside your customer's organization your software can help with, for example), you should hand the information to the sales or account management team to pursue. I have seen companies use CRMs like Salesforce to do this, but I've also seen companies input their data into a shared spreadsheet or form.

From a management perspective, it doesn't matter how you share information, just that you do and that you have a process you maintain. Sales and customer success should be very well connected and should collaborate weekly. They should meet to discuss in person or over the phone and refrain from discussing CSQLs over email.

When it comes to CSQLs, clearly define the roles and responsibilities for both the customer success and sales teams. There will be some initial confusion until you get in the groove, but if you delineate the roles, there will be less conflict while you're figuring it all out. You also want to define the roles so the sales team knows they aren't competing with customer success. Sales still gets credit for the sale because they have quotas to hit. Customer success isn't tied to a sales quota and thus shouldn't care about getting credit for the sale. Customer success is measured by metrics tied to the customer's (yep, you guessed it) success. Expansion is one clear indicator of a CSM's proficiency, but there are others—advocacy, for example.

I do believe, however, that you would do well to incentivize your customer success team. While at Looker, we paid our CSMs a sales performance incentive fund (SPIFF) on every CSQL that sales closed. It wasn't part of our formal comp plan and they certainly didn't have any quotas (I didn't want to penalize them in any way), but it rewarded our CSMs to capture and measure CSQLs. As a customer success leader, internally I am interested in maximizing my team's visibility and impact as a growth engine. Incentivizing them motivates them to look harder for expansion opportunities.

CSQL Simplified Process

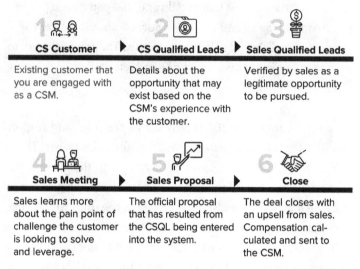

1 CS Customer	2 CS Qualified Leads	3 Sales Qualified Leads
Existing customer that you are engaged with as a CSM.	Details about the opportunity that may exist based on the CSM's experience with the customer.	Verified by sales as a legitimate opportunity to be pursued.
4 Sales Meeting	5 Sales Proposal	6 Close
Sales learns more about the pain point of challenge the customer is looking to solve and leverage.	The official proposal that has resulted from the CSQL being entered into the system.	The deal closes with an upsell from sales. Compensation calculated and sent to the CSM.

www.cspillars.com

CUSTOMER SUCCESS AS A GROWTH ENGINE

When you don't use a sales tool or a sales process for CSQLs, they get lost. I promise you, sales cares about each and every lead you send them, but if you use email to communicate (as opposed to a CRM system), your lead could get lost. Sales could be focused on another lead (or ten), and your email could get arbitrarily deprioritized. By the time they get to it, the opportunity has passed. If you don't operationalize CSQLs, not only is it frustrating for you, but you also put sales at a disadvantage. Overall, it creates a poor experience for the customer, which can translate to a lost revenue opportunity or worse, churn.

Once you as the CSM have captured the CSQL, you need to measure its impact. After it's set up in the CRM system, you can track the tangible impact of the lead. *How many additional licenses was sales able to sell? Were they able to sell the CFO on implementing our solution for the finance department?*

Measuring CSQLs also highlights when a lead *isn't* being worked. Maybe the account management team is swamped. Maybe sales is focused on other deals. Whatever the reason, when your CSQL is in a CRM, you can see whether it's being pursued. If the sales team follows up with only 80% of your CSQLs, you can hold them accountable.

You also want to measure CSQLs because it's an opportunity to expose customer success as not only a growth engine but as one of the greatest lead-generating and revenue-producing departments in the entire organization. You can literally put a number on it. "Did you realize that 30% of our revenue expansion was generated by the customer success management team?" A statement like that blows people's minds.

It also opens doors. A success team can now have a conversation with the CEO or the CFO and say, "Look at all this money the company is spending on marketing and sales, when the customer success team is generating millions of dollars of expanded revenue and is underfunded. If we could add 20% to 25% additional capacity to that team, imagine how much expansion revenue it would generate."

Capturing and measuring CSQLs allows us to verticalize, create additional tiers of expertise, and capitalize on the growth engine embedded in our customer base. And we can do it without sales quotas. If we keep the customer success team resourced with the tools and technology they need, every CSM can execute this customer success vision of expansion.

THE FOUR PHASES OF EXPANSION STRATEGY DEVELOPMENT

Now for the good stuff—how to develop a winning customer success expansion strategy. As I see it, there are four main phases.

1. **Identify and engage the stakeholders.** Identify your stakeholders (you should already have done this in your Customer Success Plan) and communicate with them regularly. Share information about customer health and customer risk. Share your Customer Success Plan. Do everything we've talked about in the Onboarding Pillar to build trust, develop a relationship, and create more interest.
2. **Identify priorities and areas of improvement.** Here, you're learning the customer's current priority. You're observing your customer's challenges and familiarizing yourself with market trends. You're looking at research and use cases. Basically, you're creating a knowledge base in your mind in order to better help the customer.
3. **Share (uptell) your research and findings with the customer.** If you find genuine areas of improvement, share them with the customer. Share market trends and industry success stories. You may even want to introduce them to another customer who can provide a positive reference. You're trying to validate the information you've gathered to create business imperative and get the customer interested in additional products or services.
4. **Confirm financial viability and capture the CSQL.** Once you've generated genuine interest from your customer and have confirmed budget availability, create a CSQL. This moves the customer into the sales cycle.

The strategy is pretty simple if you think about it. Know the stakeholder, identify priorities and room for improvement, connect the stakeholder to your findings, and bring in sales. There is no upselling and/or cross-selling—there is only up*telling*. You are explaining to your customer the opportunity they have to see increased value through the use of your solutions.

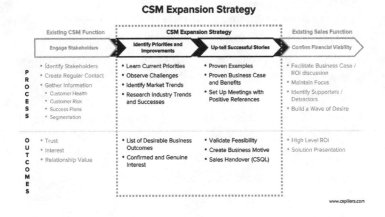

CSM Expansion Strategy

	Existing CSM Function	CSM Expansion Strategy		Existing Sales Function
	Engage Stakeholders	Identify Priorities and Improvements	Up-tell Successful Stories	Confirm Financial Viability
P R O C E S S	• Identify Stakeholders • Create Regular Contact • Gather Information • Customer Health • Customer Risk • Success Plans • Segmentation	• Learn Current Priorities • Observe Challenges • Identify Market Trends • Research Industry Trends and Successes	• Proven Examples • Proven Business Case and Benefits • Set Up Meetings with Positive References	• Facilitate Business Case / ROI discussion • Maintain Focus • Identify Supporters / Detractors • Build a Wave of Desire
O U T C O M E S	• Trust • Interest • Relationship Value	• List of Desirable Business Outcomes • Confirmed and Genuine Interest	• Validate Feasibility • Create Business Motive • Sales Handover (CSQL)	• High Level ROI • Solution Presentation

www.cspillars.com

HOW CAN OUR TOOLBOX HELP?

You can round out your customer expansion strategies using the Customer Success Toolbox.

MOMENTS OF TRUTH

Moments of truth have been critical in the Onboarding, Adoption, and Retention Pillars and continue to be in expansion.

How are you continuing to provide value to your customer? Are you continuing to ensure other teams (such as marketing, finance, engineering, etc.) are properly supporting the customer? Are these departments still living up to their end of the bargain and creating outstanding moments of truth?

As you've done in other pillars, make sure you identify each moment of truth in the Expansion Pillar and keep your finger on the pulse.

PLAYBOOKS

There are seven playbooks I recommend for the Expansion Pillar and four you should start right away. These playbooks are internally focused and should be formulaic and easy. They can even be automated.

1. How CSMs and Renewal Managers (if they are separate people) Work Together for Customer Renewals
2. How to Uptell
3. How to Cross-Sell from the Perspective of Uptelling
4. How to Connect Your Company's Capabilities to Your Customer's Problems

Creating these playbooks means bridging the gap between your company's capabilities and the customer's problem. It means partnering with product marketing and understanding the solutions your peers are developing. It also means understanding other customers in the same industry or with the same product line.

Once those playbooks are underway, I also recommend building a playbook for trial conversions, price increases, and multiyear conversions.

CUSTOMER HEALTH

Think back to the way we measure customer health. In the Expansion Pillar, we want the customer's product usage, business outcome, and customer feedback indicators to be very strong. If they are, customer expansion is more likely.

CUSTOMER RISK

Feature risk is the risk to focus on in the Expansion Pillar, and as we've seen with other risks, there is an acute and persistent version.

- **Acute feature risk:** This occurs when a customer buys your product and doesn't get access to a feature (or features) they were promised. Maybe the feature was pushed out. Maybe there was an issue with it. Maybe it was scrapped altogether or just plain forgotten. Regardless of the reason, the customer will likely leave to find another solution to their problem because they can't wait any longer. They need a solution to their problem *now*.
- **Persistent feature risk:** Acute risk is definitely something to make note of, but it's really persistent feature risk that we need to keep our eye on. If a customer continually asks for features and you don't respond to their ideas, or complains repetitively about the same glitch that never gets fixed, eventually they will leave. Instead, they will go to where they feel heard and where they can influence the product roadmap.

So what does this mean for customer success professionals? We need to track our customers' feature ideas and collate them. Every customer success organization should have a methodology or process to organize and prioritize feature ideas. Otherwise, you're pitching individual feature ideas for individual customers, which is much harder for the engineering and product teams to process.

You also want to communicate with your customers about their ideas because you want them to know you're listening and trying to help them get what they need to succeed. Communicate with them. A customer would rather hear no than feel ignored.

CUSTOMER SUCCESS PLAN

Throughout the customer's journey, we have been tracking a lot of different metrics. Did we drive to value one during onboarding? Did we achieve operational dependence during adoption? During retention, did we get the customer to renew? In the Expansion Pillar, the main focus of the Customer Success Plan is to identify customer champions to help determine the customer's real problems.

A stakeholder generally knows the overarching business strategies and the goals the company is trying to achieve. Customer champions are typically inside the business on the front lines. They know which problems need to be solved to make their lives easier. These are tactical employees who are looking at day-to-day operations. They continually ask themselves, *what do we need to help us do our jobs?*

Customer champions are great resources to tap into. You can work with them to determine additional value you can drive, and you can use your previous Customer Success Plan wins to help uptell.

Finally, sometimes customers want to see additional use cases. If a customer wants to learn more about X, you need to research X and present your findings to the customer. The findings will hopefully get them further interested in your product and then converted to a CSQL. All of this should go into your Customer Success Plan.

WHAT TO TRACK IN YOUR CUSTOMER SUCCESS PLAN

There are two expansion metrics you should track in your Customer Success Plan, and the first is time to expansion (TTE). Sometimes customer buying patterns emerge—a customer buys a specific product, and then 12 months later, they buy a complementary product because they understand the value and want to buy more. If you have a data and analytics team, ask them to run an analysis to provide expansion indicators so you have an idea of when to uptell your customers.

The second metric you want to track is average expansion size (AES). What does expansion typically look like for the product during this part of the life cycle or in that region of the world? Understanding this metric allows us to see and realize potential opportunities, which helps with forecasting. It starts to formalize metrics around the "land and expand" concept that everyone talks about but doesn't really understand how effective they are at it.

SEGMENTATION

You should always segment between industries, products, and geographies, but in the Expansion Pillar, you also want to segment historical expansion so you can identify trends. The segmentation can help to classify the use cases and identify references to leverage during uptelling.

METRICS

Metrics that focus on GRR and NRR are obvious, but with this pillar, we also want to augment these with newer metrics including TTE, AES, and CSQLs. And when it comes to CSQLs, you can go a level deeper tracking the number of CSQLs, how many close, the time to close, and so on. And don't forget to ask the data analysts for insight on expansion patterns within your customer base.

TIPS AND TRICKS FOR EXPANSION

Are you ready for some pro tips on how to improve expansion? Do I even have to ask?

1. PRODUCT MARKETING IS YOUR BEST FRIEND.

If you don't know every product, every feature, and every use case, you're missing out on an opportunity to help your customer. You're doing them a disservice. Work with product marketing to create training materials geared toward CSMs. The most consequential thing is understanding all the solutions your company has to offer. If you're a one-product company, you easily know your product inside and out. Uptelling new features and services is simple. But if you work for a massive company like Google which has hundreds of products, you don't necessarily need to learn them all, but you *do* need to be able to access case studies and solutions quickly and easily in case you're asked.

2. UNDERSTAND THE CUSTOMER'S VISION.

Do whatever you can to fully understand your customer's vision of the future and do even more to help get them there. Use your industry knowledge and/or your knowledge of other customers in the same space doing similar things. Educate yourself on everything related to your customer in order to help them solve their problems.

3. KEEP UP THE PACE AND MOMENTUM.

If you've done a great job during onboarding, adoption, and retention, leverage that momentum during uptelling. If you tell the customer they will have even more success, they will be excited. This has nothing to do with selling more software or services—this is about using momentum to reach the desired outcomes of both parties.

4. KNOW THE EXPANSION PATTERNS.

This ties into the metrics you want to track in your Customer Success Plan—TTE and AES. If you know your customer's expansion patterns, you can proactively leverage them to uptell your customer base.

THOUGHT LEADERSHIP SERIES: MATT COLLIER

Next up in the Thought Leadership Series, we hear from **Matt Collier, Head of Customer Success and Growth (Americas), Digital Experience, at Adobe.** *I met Matt many years ago and immediately recognized him as an innovative and forward-thinking customer success leader. And when it came to leveraging customer success for expansion and partnering with marketing, it was clear he knew more than me about this essential concept. Enjoy.*

EXPANSION: DELIVERING STRATEGIC VALUE

As Marketo (acquired by Adobe in 2018) continued to grow, one of our strategic objectives was to increase our net retention rate, specifically the amount of expansion revenue from our customer base. To achieve this share-of-wallet objective in the competitive martech space, we needed strong customer adoption as a prerequisite and had to build on that with an entirely differentiated customer experience. We took two critical steps. First, we partnered with our marketing team to better understand our customer base through the creation of an "expansion" ideal customer profile (ICP) based on a look-alike model of customers that had previously purchased, combined with other insights that would indicate their growth. Second, we transformed our organizational model by creating new customer segmentation, allowing us to fund a dedicated sales team to prioritize high-value opportunities, as well as centralizing the entire organization around a methodology focused on our customers' success. Both the creation of this propensity-to-buy metric, or expansion ICP, and operating model and engagement methodology, allowed us to provide customers with a prescriptive and strategic engagement, driving expansion revenue and net retention, and a much better customer and employee experience.

The creation of our expansion ICP started with analyzing our customer data: looking for correlations between previous purchasers and existing customers, creating a look-alike scoring metric. This included everything from industry, company size (revenue, head count), growth rates (employees, database/usage), other technologies in use, our own product adoption metric, company location, and so forth. We then added on top a layer of third-party data to enrich this dataset, including social media insights, hiring trends, funding raised, website content, employee and executive turnover, and so on. Combined, this allowed us to further narrow the parameters for customers that should be a strong fit within our product's use case. This allowed us to create a fairly confident scoring mechanism for propensity to buy, which we could then segment into expansion ICP groupings and prioritize our engagements.

However, if our new expansion ICP was rolled out within our same operating and customer engagement model, our teams would still struggle to provide a truly differentiated customer experience. First, rolling out updated customer segments, with improved automation and efficiencies, allowed us to better allocate resources, freeing up operational expenses to fund a dedicated sales team. Second, we rolled out a new organization-wide value-based selling methodology focused on providing prescriptive advice based on our customer's business objectives, including current adoption level and value realized, in advance of any customer engagement. This required bandwidth to conduct research, build an account plan, align other functions, and perform at the executive level. With this investment into our customer's success done in advance, we successfully positioned ourselves as strategic partners who could help customers unlock more value with their existing platform and include additional functionality.

Overall, to grow revenue from our customer base required that we change ourselves. We needed to better understand our customers with a data-driven approach in a large volume and velocity environment and we needed to change how we provided value by unequivocally focusing on our customer's objectives. The lagging indicators justified the change: improved opportunity creation, win rates, average contract values, expansion, and net retention. Perhaps more impactful but less tangible are the benefits this prioritization and focus provided better employee experiences and stronger customer relationships, which will pay many dividends to come.

THE MAIN EVENT

In the Ironman of customer success, the main event is expansion. It's what you've been training for all year. You worked hard on onboarding, kept your head down during adoption, and showed real grit to get the renewal. You successfully navigated the training program and made it to expansion.

To remind you, Patrick Campbell, the CEO of ProfitWell, said, "Data suggests customer success impacts expansion more than gross churn." In the past, retention was the focus of customer success, but as we've talked about a lot throughout this book, that focus has evolved. Today, customer success is viewed as a growth engine for expansion, and the renewal has become the entry fee to the main event.

If expansion is the main event, advocacy is the winner's circle. We'll talk more about that next.

CHAPTER 8

PILLAR #6: ADVOCACY

"VALUE CHAMPIONED"

The Seven Customer Success Pillars

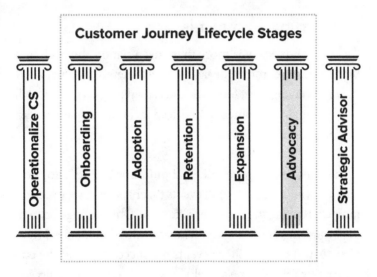

www.cspillars.com

Yesterday, I had a conversation with one of my biggest custom-ers about their advocacy program. They are a $1 billion company with thousands of clients.

"We have a ton of advocates," the stakeholder responded. "We always get thank-you notes and emails. And we have internal case studies and testimonials."

"Wow, that's great," I said. "Do you capture that feedback and share it with the market?"

"Oh, no. We don't do that."

"Then you don't have customer advocacy."

"What do you mean?" the stakeholder asked.

"You have advocates, but you aren't leveraging them for advocacy."

A PROFESSIONAL PAT ON THE BACK

Customer advocacy is more than just a pat on the back or a thank-you note from your satisfied customers. Customer advocacy is receiving great feedback and capitalizing on it. I can't tell you how many customer success leaders (and company leadership in general) miss this.

Up to this point, we've talked about onboarding, adoption, retention, and expansion, all events that happen at very specific moments during the customer's life cycle. Onboarding occurs at the beginning of the engagement, and adoption happens right after that. If both of those events are successful (and the customer sees future value as well), next up is retention, followed by expansion. They all flow together quite nicely.

But the Advocacy Pillar is different. Customer advocacy can

happen at any point throughout the customer's life cycle, and so it transcends all the other pillars.

Here's my definition.

> Customer advocacy is a competitive advantage for your company because it assists in the acquisition of new logos and solidifies existing customers through a multitude of assets and programs.

How can customer advocacy create a *competitive advantage*? It's like reading a review before you buy something. The more advocates you have spreading the word, the more evidence you have that your solution works.

The next part of the definition—*assisting in the acquisition of new logos*—refers to a sales process. Today, the buying process has shifted the power to the consumer. Peer reviews and online review sites such as Trust Radius, G2, and Gartner are exploding, and these companies thrive by reviewing companies, publishing reports, and advising customers. It's easy these days for customers to gain insight and understanding about the quality of your product. They can bypass marketing and go straight to the people who actually use it. Having strong advocates prominent in the marketplace is key to the acquisition of new logos.

Customer advocacy also *solidifies existing customers*. If you have a customer who is struggling to find value, send them another customer's success story. When they see it, they are likely to shift their thinking. *Why isn't that working for us? What are we doing differently?* It may be that you discover you're doing something wrong, as opposed to your customer, but sharing a success story gets that conversation started.

A multitude of customer programs and assets speaks to how broad customer advocacy manifests itself in the marketplace. Every customer success organization should have programs and assets in place to drive advocacy, but (it seems silly that I even have to say this) remember to keep them about the customer, not your solution. If you try to force or manipulate advocacy to tell a specific story, it will come across as inauthentic.

WHO CARES?

Customer advocacy matters to every business organization because it helps us acquire new logos and solidify existing customers. It's also compelling in that it's the new way companies create value for their customers and drive growth for their own organizations. Ultimately, there are five benefits to customer advocacy.

1. **It gives you a competitive advantage.** We talked about this in the previous section, but ultimately, customer advocacy is proof your product or service delivers on its promise. It tells your prospects your solution works, and they can have confidence in partnering with your organization for success.
2. **It accelerates deal cycles.** Let's say you have a prospect who is on the fence because they are weighing multiple options. Customer advocacy can cut through the noise so a decision can be made faster. "Yes, we want that experience. That's exactly what we need. We want that outcome."
3. **It helps with retention.** If you want to do well in the Retention Pillar (why wouldn't you, now that you have access to the seven pillars?), customer advocacy can give you a leg up.

When customers struggle to see value, it gives them pause. Customer advocacy shows them your solution *can* have an impact, which sparks an authentic conversation about why they aren't getting the same result.

4. **It helps with expansion.** When customers look at new case studies of alternative use cases, attend a webinar on another customer's success, or read an online review or announcement email, they get new ideas or realize they too need that capability. "We want that, too. We *need* that, too! Can we have it now?" Customer advocacy drives expansion.

5. **It gives you insights.** Customer advocacy also tells you what the customer is really thinking. Remember the online reviews or testimonials you've read. Are they all positive? Are they all negative? Or are they a little bit of both? I have found customers are honest and real about what they like and don't like (and what they like and don't like from your competitors as well), which gives you tremendous insight. You can find out where your competitors are weak and you are strong, and vice versa.

Not only does customer advocacy give you a competitive advantage, but it also accelerates deal cycles, helps with retention and expansion, and gives you insights.

But how important is it to customer success?

WHY DOES ADVOCACY MATTER TO CUSTOMER SUCCESS, THEN?

Advocacy is an extension of what CSMs already do. Customer success teams work hard to create and nurture long-term relationships with their customers because they are responsible for monitoring the customer experience throughout their journey.

They're in the best position to identify and reach out to customers they feel have adopted the product, enjoy it, and see value.

You likely already have these assets and programs in place, but I want to caution you: for most companies, these assets and programs aren't formalized or rigorous. Many of the customer success and C-suite leaders I talk to will say, "We have case studies, testimonials, and referrals. Check, check, check," but all they're doing is going through the motions and checking off boxes. They don't really understand what the asset or program is, what it's trying to achieve, or the operational discipline needed to make it valuable.

Remember that billion-dollar company I mentioned earlier? I also talked to them about their advocacy assets.

"Yeah, we have case studies. We do all of that."

"How many products do you have as a company?" I asked.

"Forty or so."

"And how many case studies do you have?"

There was a pause. "We have 47 case studies."

"You have customers around the world, in over 100 different countries, and 40 products that can each do a multitude of different things, yet you have only *47 case studies*?" I asked.

"Oh, is that low?"

"Absolutely, that's low!" I said. "How many CSMs do you have?"

"Two hundred fifty."

"If every CSM is responsible for producing one case study, that's already a huge multiplication on what you currently have. And if you think about multiple assets for each customer—online reviews, testimonials, referrals—you really should have thousands of case studies, not 47."

When the conversation first started, the billion-dollar company believed they had an adequate number of case studies. They were ready to place a check mark in that box. They quickly found out, however, that their efforts were falling short. It was clear they had a huge opportunity to make their case study efforts truly valuable.

SO WHAT ASSETS DO WE NEED?

To leverage the benefits of customer advocacy, we have to enable our customers to advocate for our business, and we want to make their efforts valuable. There are a number of different methodologies you can tap into to achieve that, but I have found there are five main assets each customer success organization needs.

1. VALUE ASSESSMENTS AND MATURITY ASSESSMENTS

Value Assessments: Case studies are only one of the assets that drive advocacy. But before you can get to them, you first need a value assessment to confirm you have driven to value and delivered the customer's desired outcome.

Value assessments help with retention and expansion. They can also help with onboarding and adoption. Value assessments provide quantifiable feedback on the impact of your solution that can quickly be turned into additional assets. For example, if 87% of your customers see a 30% revenue increase after using your product or service, your marketing department can develop a campaign highlighting that.

Mature companies are great at collating their value assessments to create infographics and cull phrases they can include in presentations, brochures, and on their websites. This content is measured, real, and impactful and makes it easier to demonstrate that you as an organization have driven to value. Once you do, asking for a testimonial (or permission to use your customer in a case study) is much easier and more effective.

Maturity Assessments: This is an excellent way to benchmark your customer's journey with your solution. We as customer success leaders (and future leaders) have taken those customer success maturity assessments online, so we know they can take on a variety of focuses. For example, ESG has a maturity assessment[14] that measures the journey from build to operationalize to transform, TSIA uses the standard forming, storming, norming, and performing[15] way teams need to mature to advance, as developed by Dr. Bruce Tuckman in the 1960s,[16] or Gainsights assessment that tracks based on the evolution of the success team—reactive, informed, proactive, and predictive. Your job is to build the model that matches what your customer journeys look like as they go from new to the gold standard in

---

14 Sheik Ayube, "The Customer Success Maturity Model," ESG, April 1, 2020, https://esgsuccess.com/the-customer-success-maturity-model/.

15 Phil Nanus, "The Customer Success Maturity Model in 4 Phases," TSIA, accessed January 14, 2021, https://www.tsia.com/blog/4-phases-of-customer-success-maturity.

16 Judith Stein, "Using the Stages of Team Development," MIT Human Resources, accessed January 14, 2021, https://hr.mit.edu/learning-topics/teams/articles/stages-development.

customers. No matter what you build, they are all valid. Some are more valuable, but ultimately, they are a way to see where your customer is in their maturity. If they're far enough along the curve, they can be used to encourage, motivate, and inspire other customers along their journey.

2. USER-GENERATED CONTENT

The next asset you should focus on is user-generated content. These are usually testimonials, online reviews, and case studies.

Testimonials and Online Reviews

These assets play a crucial part because they allow you to benchmark yourself against your competitors. *How do your products, service, and prices compare?*

You can also "strut without strutting" with testimonials and online reviews, allowing you to boast about the quality of your service and the effectiveness of the solution (or how awesome it is to work with you), all without coming across as an egotistical maniac. You can brag about your skills because it isn't you who is doing the actual bragging. Your customer is doing it for you.

Finally, testimonials and reviews provide insight and firsthand knowledge of your customers' likes, dislikes, recommendations, and benefits. You can use online reviews, for example, to see your customers' perceptions of your products. *Where do you really shine? Where do you fall short?*

Testimonials and online reviews are a great way to foster advocacy, but make sure you have a recommendation program in place. In the SaaS world, most recommendations are done either in person or by word of mouth, but a strategic recommendation program can change the process for the better. So home in on your advocates and be proactive. Tell them exactly where to leave their online review and encourage them to record a video testimonial. Don't expect anyone to carve out time to do that for you. They may be advocates, but they're still busy with full calendars. Have a program in place and proactively approach your customers to get the review done. And remember to thank the customer for doing so.

Case Studies

Case studies are next-level thinking. Also a user-generated asset, they exist to tell your customers the value of your solution in story form—they enable your customer to talk about the value they've realized from working with you by painting a detailed, picturesque story about their experience. These stories can cover anything from impeccable implementation, to excellent customer support, to driving value and achieving the customer's desired outcome.

Typically, marketing will write the case study (they have the templates and skills to capture, write, and publish written content). However, the CSM is the best person to *identify* the case study opportunity and capture information to include with it. The CSM will get the approvals from the customer to do the case study and make the introduction to marketing. The CSM will also provide a short written summary of the facts so marketing isn't going in blind. The CSM will also ensure the appropriate thank-you is delivered.

I know what you're thinking: *That sounds like hard work.* But I promise you, it isn't. Case studies are inexpensive and easy to do. They take anywhere from 10 to 20 hours to build and deploy and can be delivered as a PDF, blog article, video clip, or infographic. And naturally, if multiple people are working on it, the process moves even faster.

I use five components to build an effective case study. After you've written a few with the same simple template, you'll become more proficient—and prolific—in creating them.

1. **Describe the state of the industry/market before your solution came along.** Set the scene and highlight the issues and challenges (potentially with a competitor) that existed before you entered the marketplace. By default, you're saying that by working with you, these issues and challenges were solved.

2. **Explain the implementation experience as well as the valuable capabilities of the product.** For example, software implementation is always difficult and challenging. No one likes to do them. We all start with high hopes, but things inevitably go downhill. A case study about implementation would help prospects understand what it's like to do one with your company. If your prospect reads a case study about software implementation, they will get an understanding of how the process works, that you know what you're doing, that you've had success. Case studies tell your prospects that your product or service works.

3. **Discuss improvements in numbers and metrics that quantify the desired outcome and value being attained.** These days, data drives decisions, so we need to make sure we include defensible numbers in our case studies as much as possible. In the old days, you could get away with skipping over the numbers: "We saw a huge increase in usage last quarter." But that doesn't work today. People want to know

the specific numbers and understand how those numbers were derived.

4. **Celebrate the success and focus on what's happening next.** Remember when I said people don't renew with you because of what you've done in the past but based on your vision of the future? Advocates not only talk about their amazing experiences and terrific outcomes, but they also talk about the future. This is the icing on the cake of your case study because it reveals the customer is willing to expand their relationship with you. They're willing to go deeper and spend more, which is a huge, positive sign.

5. **Partner with marketing to appropriately package and deploy the case study.** It sounds silly, but make sure the tone and style are correct and the images speak to the essence of the case study. Be thoughtful about what you include in the document. Don't include generic, stock photos of diverse people sitting around a conference room talking. If the image doesn't gel with the content of the case study, leave it out.

In my opinion, case studies aren't overly difficult. Once your customer agrees to do one (and the seven pillars help you get to this piece of the equation easier), the CSM will then provide the overview to marketing and then bring marketing into the conversation. And if your customer wants their identity or brand protected, no problem. There are many ways you can keep your customers' identity anonymous. You can mention the industry they're in, the size of their organization, or that they are a *Fortune* 100 company, as examples.

Just remember to keep the case study about the customer. I can't reiterate that enough. It's about *their* journey and *their* story. It features *their* skills, capabilities, and decision making. A good case study isn't about writing a ten-page diatribe about how great your product is. If you try to influence the case study, it will reek of inauthenticity.

3. CUSTOMER REFERRALS

The third asset every customer success organization should have in their advocacy back pocket is customer referrals. Sales and marketing are responsible for lead development and new business, which can get quite costly. It's expensive to attract new customers, but referrals are free. Referrals may come into you cold, but when one CEO asks another CEO what software they use, it's invaluable. This "hidden" word-of-mouth referral is common, but because it typically happens without our direct awareness, we sometimes forget its impact. A great advocacy program will ensure customer referrals happen in the background, hidden from our immediate view.

We also tend to forget the online reviews our customers write are *amplified* referrals—dozens, hundreds, or even *thousands* of prospects will read them *as if they were a referral*. We need to remember to pay attention to them, too.

Alternatively, you can ask a customer to be an *active* referral and speak to an indecisive prospect directly.

To the prospect, you'll say, "I know you're on the fence and can't decide whether to pull the trigger on this new product. Would you like to speak to someone else in your industry who has seen the same challenges and used our product to overcome them?"

Ninety-nine times out of 100, the prospect will say, "Absolutely." Then, once you have sign off from the prospect, go back to your customer advocate and ask them to do a referral call.

Referrals work. Nielsen did a study that found people are four times more likely to buy a product when it's referred to them by someone they know and trust.[17] That's a pretty good statistic. *The Journal of Marketing* released another study that claimed a referred customer has a 16% higher lifetime value than customers acquired through other methods.[18]

Both studies back up my experience: SaaS businesses benefit greatly from references and testimonials. Conversion rates increase dramatically, and it makes the selling process (particularly closing) a lot simpler and easier for your team. Today, people like to follow influencers and listen to their recommendations. Social media provides another way to put testimonials in front of the prospect; add relevant customer quotes to your website, Twitter profile, or LinkedIn page.

Customer Reference Library

We can also increase our number of customer references.

I recommend creating a customer reference library to ensure your team is tracking how often references are being used. I have seen companies repeatedly ask the same three customers for a reference simply because they didn't have a system to track their requests.

When I was a customer of Salesforce, I must have been asked to do a dozen reference calls in three months. I'm always happy

---

17   "Under the Influence: Consumer Trust in Advertising," Nielsen, September 17, 2013, https://www.nielsen.com/us/en/insights/article/2013/under-the-influence-consumer-trust-in-advertising/.

18   Phillip Schmitt, Bernd Skiera, and Christophe van den Bulte, "Referral Programs and Customer Value," *The Journal of Marketing* 75 (2011): 46–59, https://doi.org/10.2307/25764294.

to help, but it's a bit much to ask the same person to take 30 minutes to an hour out of their day to be a reference for your company multiple times a quarter.

Over time, once you've amassed a bunch of referrals, you can start to group them by industry, geography, company size, use case, outcomes, metrics, and so forth, and your library becomes a long-term strategic asset. To make your library a long-term strategic asset, you will need enough referrals that will allow you to slice and dice them into a number of categories such as industry, geography, company size, use case, outcomes, metrics, and so on. The more the better.

Not only are customer referrals more affordable than traditional new customer acquisition, but they're also more effective. Advisor Impact conducted a study on customer referrals and found 83% of satisfied customers are willing to refer your company to their peers.[19] That's astounding!

But the study also found that only 23% of those customers actually do.[20] The vast majority of satisfied customers are willing to be a customer referral, but only a handful are realized.

Why?

It's because most companies don't have a formal customer reference program or a formal referral program. By simply having a program and tracking our referrals, we can increase that percentage and our number of customer references.

19 "Stop Avoiding Referrals—5 Painless Ways to Increase Your Referrals Today—Salesperson," incentivefox.com, December 15, 2017, https://www.incentivefox.com/blog/2017/12/11/stop-avoiding-referrals-5-painless-ways-to-increase-your-referrals-today-salesperson.

20 "Stop Avoiding Referrals."

4. REFERRING AS OPPOSED TO A REFERRAL

The fourth asset is something I call referring as opposed to referral. The words are very similar, but to me, there is a definite distinction. *Referring* is when an advocate leaves the company you're currently servicing, goes to a different company, and refers you in. "I used this product at my last company, and it was amazing. We should use it here, too. Let me contact my old CSM and schedule a quick chat." A *referral* is when you ask a customer to speak to a specific prospect.

Referring is advocacy gold because you don't have to do any outreach. The customer advocate literally reaches out to explain the problem that you probably helped solved for them in the past.

How do you acquire this asset? By cultivating your customer champions throughout their customer journey.

5. FOCUSED EVENTS

The last asset every customer success organization should have are focused events. One of the best aspects of any advocacy program is the ability to elevate the advocate both inside and *outside* their company. You can do this through speaking engagements and trade shows, and even prospect, industry, and customer appreciation events (in person or online). Whatever the medium, focused events give you the opportunity to showcase your advocate positively and help elevate their career.

Every year, I invite external customers to an internal customer success summit (think sales kickoff but for customer success), which brings together the entire internal customer success organization (including support, renewals, professional services, customer success management, and training and certification).

They weren't employees, but I asked them to take part in the summit to not only tell their story (the good and the bad) but also to help.

When we create our customer journey maps, we think we know what the customer is doing based on our experience. A focused event allows you to gain insights into your customers' real experiences, as well as amplify the power of your advocacy program.

WHAT ABOUT ADVOCACY PROGRAMS?

At a minimum, we need those five assets. In conjunction, we also need the three Cs: customer advisory boards (CABs), champions, and communities (specifically, *online* customer communities). Most advocacy programs I've seen have one or two of these elements, but if you want to maximize your efforts and really capitalize on your advocates, you need them all.

CUSTOMER ADVISORY BOARD

I highly recommend every customer success organization have a number of CABs. At these events, you can talk about the present and the future. *How can we provide our customers with even more value? How can we get better?* These are fantastic questions for your customer advisors to answer and provide insight on.

What I just described will work, but to really excel, I suggest going deeper. If you're a CSM and you have enough customers in your portfolio (5 to 15 should work), I think you should have your *own* CAB. Find a commonality—such as product, vertical/horizontal, industry, or geography—and connect your customers. Talk about what works and what doesn't work. Talk about the features they love and the features they could do without.

Make your advisory board diverse. Stack it with super-advocates as well as with customers who are struggling. When the struggling customers hear from the successful customers, they'll take a step back and think, *We're missing something here. We should be getting that value, too.* Struggling customers will feel stronger about their possibility of success with you, so bring them in as well as advocates.

If you have a big enough customer portfolio, you can even have different advisory boards representing different demographics. Most companies only have a CAB representative of their fanciest clients (and every company certainly should have at least that), but if you stop there, you're missing an opportunity to attain 360-degree information. Whatever you decide to do, develop a strong program around running and maintaining your CABs.

CHAMPION PROGRAM

Next, you need champions. You want to find people who have a strong passion for your product, want to see it succeed, and are willing to help see everything around implementation or adoption, for example, done properly. These are the people you need to find and support.

When you find someone who is passionate about driving your solution, give them as much insight as you can around your solution's best practices. Send them case studies and white papers, anything that helps them understand what's possible with your solution. Build a playbook for champions, too. Give them visibility on future product roadmaps or advocacy opportunities. For example, tell them, "We're at a conference later this year. Would you be interested in speaking about our product?"

You also want to keep your champions up to date on your solution. When I was at Salesforce, I lobbied to give all our biggest champions (we called them MVPs) free training and certifications. I didn't expect our champions to pay to stay certified and current on our products.

And don't forget to nurture them. We also gave our champions swag to wear and distribute, as well as priority status and seating at corporate events. This is how you turn these champions into external advocates, which is the goal.

Despite the benefits of creating a champion program, few companies formalize it. They know who their champions are and will give them swag and send them white papers every now and then, but a formal platform gives your champions access to training, visibility, programs, *and* did I mention swag? There's a growing movement to eliminate swag in favor of more altruistic offerings (such as donating to the champion's favorite nonprofit). I believe there is room for both in this world.

It's like membership to an exclusive club. Make admission to your champion program valid for 6 to 12 months. "In order to qualify again, you need to do these things for us." When you make it a program, you can scale it, operationalize it, automate it, track it, and measure it.

ADVOCACY MATURITY MAP™

I've spent a lot of time talking about the different advocacy assets and programs every customer success organization should have, but I haven't told you how to find your advocates and get them to advocate for you. Let's do that now.

Running an advocacy program is different than simply having a bunch of advocates in your corner. Remember that story I told you at the beginning of the chapter; an advocacy program means capitalizing on your advocates. It also means working with an advocate maturity map, a process I've created to determine how to best move your advocates through your advocacy program.

Advocacy Maturity Map

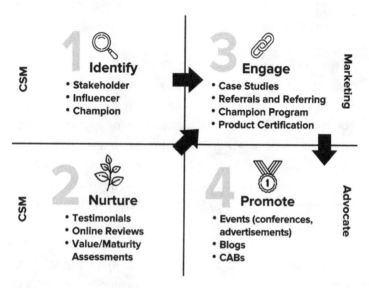

www.cspillars.com

1. Identify the Advocate

There are four steps to developing an effective advocate maturity map, and the first is to identify the advocate. This will be someone within your customer's organization who would make a terrific advocate. It could be the stakeholder, but it could also be an influencer or product champion.

Sometimes, identifying the advocate is easy because they will tell you directly; "I love working with you guys. You make everything so *easy*. If there's anything I can do to help you, please let me know." But sometimes, it's especially difficult, too. I have found this happens when the CSM hasn't spent time thinking about who the advocate could be. You may also target an individual to be an advocate using the maturity roadmap, but of course, it's so much easier when they present themselves to you.

2. Nurture the Advocate

Once you identify the advocate, you have to *nurture* them. Create a value assessment and share it with them: "Look at how much value I'm driving for you." You're priming them to become an advocate because they will want to tell their internal teams how much revenue growth or cost savings they made by working with you. They made the smart decision to work with you as a vendor—the value assessment will not only prime them for advocacy, but it will also personally benefit them. They are more likely to give an online review or testimonial at this stage.

Please keep in mind, however, that nurturing doesn't stop once you move to the next phase of the map. Don't make that mistake. If they give you a testimonial, for example, you need to thank them for their time by sending them a thank-you card (handwritten) or gift card. You can talk to their boss about how great they are, and you can give them an online review. You want to continue to nurture your advocates so you can move them from minor advocacy requests such as testimonials to the case study or referral big leagues.

3. Engage the Advocate

When your advocate has been nurtured, it's time to engage them.

Here, we are looking for case studies, references, referrals, and champion programs. Value assessments (which is the consultative process of identifying the business impact of an investment in your solution as a business case, taking into account what the customer needs to achieve for success) help here, too, because they elevate your advocate's ability to sing your praises. With a value assessment, your advocate transforms into a *great* advocate because they will have the data and ROI (in hand) to back up their claims. "Not only do I love working with them, but here's also the defensible data why you should, too."

4. Promote the Advocate

After you successfully engage your advocates, you can move them to the promote stage on your advocate maturity map. It's at this stage where your advocates will go out and promote your brand online or at physical events. They will drive conversations about your brand and solution. This could be as simple as holding a brand-sponsored event (such as a hackathon) inside their own customer organization.

Who Owns the Advocate Maturity Map?

CSMs and customer marketing share responsibility for the advocate maturity map. CSMs are responsible for identifying and nurturing candidates, which makes sense. They are closest to and know the customer best. Customer marketing is best suited for the engage and promote phases because they drive the machine that can amplify the customer's message. They can make it look and sound great, and make sure it gets into the hands of the right people.

You don't necessarily need to nurture advocates to get them to the promote phase of the map. Sometimes you'll get a stake-holder who is so enamored with you that they offer to promote your brand on their own. This is the dream:

"It was fantastic working with you, and I would love to tell our story."

"Would you do a case study for us?"

"Absolutely."

But this is the exception rather than the rule. More often than not, the broader your advocacy base, the more nurture is needed.

I recommend placing your advocate maturity map in your Customer Success Plan. Make sure you've labeled the advocates you've identified, for example, versus the ones you've nurtured, engaged, or promoted.

ONLINE COMMUNITY

The online community, or more specifically, the *customer* online community, is a place where customers, partners, employees, and other product experts can come together to discuss reviews, brainstorm new product ideas, and engage with one another about our company's products and services. It's also a place to talk about business outcomes and value. You're sharing best practices and providing real-time feedback with the community.

You can start to identify new potential advocates, too. You already know how your stakeholders interact with your product, but an online community gives you additional insight. It allows you to see how other people promote your brand, and suddenly, new advocates emerge.

Customer online communities are crucial, but not every company has a "real" one. A lot of businesses have online forums, but they are used more for ticket deflections and take the pressure off the support team. Or a place to advertise new product releases. The benefit of an online community is human contact. It isn't automated. It isn't asynchronous—you're talking to real people, just like you.

THOUGHT LEADERSHIP SERIES: XINA SEATON

*I first met **Xina Seaton, VP of Customer Experience at Blue Prism**, over 20 years ago when I started working at Vignette. Since then, I've seen her follow a similar path to mine, moving from education and training to the customer success field. Xina has a customer passion that extends beyond what is considered normal, and she's driving incredible initiatives, such as Women in RPA, an organization that spotlights successful women leading the way in the emerging tech industry. Here's her take on how to build a B2B customer community in 12 months.*

REBUILDING A B2B CUSTOMER COMMUNITY IN 12 MONTHS

Social media has created new expectations for B2B businesses. Customers want the opportunity to network, learn from experts, share and discuss ideas, and contribute to the innovation and evolution of products or services. An active community enables users to help other users and self-service on issues that drive ticket deflection, improve first-time resolution, and reduce support costs. And the community is an excellent place to engage, ask, listen, and act to improve satisfaction, product adoption, and retention.

The importance of a community cannot be underestimated but can be overlooked by executives as its importance has exponentially increased over the last several years. Building the business case for an investment in a strong community can be challenging, but it is a strategic imperative. In today's experience economy where customers are faced regularly with a buy or renew decision, there is a clear connection to the company's financial performance.

Customers are eager to share what they think and how a business can serve them better, so ask, listen, and act. Having a voice of the customer program enabled us to uncover some dissatisfaction with our online user community that was unacceptable to the business and could negatively impact market perceptions if unaddressed.

We built a top five attack list:

1. Give the users a better experience and higher engagement with other users.
2. Implement a best-in-class community platform; what we had was old, clunky, and hard to use.
3. Implement a formal moderation process with an SLA to ensure all posts are answered timely.
4. Integrate our processes into other functions such as product, training, documentation, and support.
5. Grow membership; we had only 500 members visiting monthly and we restricted any access to members only.

We knew we needed to act fast and set an aggressive goal to launch a new community experience with our upcoming user conference less than six months away. To ensure we met this target, we took several actions in parallel.

First, we listened to our customers. Having received survey responses from 350 users, we interviewed 50 customers in one-on-one setting, spoke to a range of individuals internally, and built a high-level journey map identifying key pain points. This resulted in making key decisions about community platform requirements, engagement expectations, and user accessibility. We launched a search for a community manager to join the team to provide a dedicated resource to our members. This role would ensure we engaged in a timely manner, encouraged community networking, and connected internally to the teams and resources who needed to engage with our users.

Second, we took a close look at ourselves. We built a solid set of requirements and evaluated several best-in-class technology solutions in the market ultimately selecting an SaaS provider and deploying the initial revamped community experience within three months. We formed alliances with internal teams, developed internal processes, and established the links that we needed to connect the organization to the community members.

Third, we set goals.

- Reach 5,000 monthly users in six months and then double it after one year.
- Have *no* post go unanswered with a committed SLA.
- Track and measure support ticket deflection.
- Implement ideation with product team to ensure voice of customer is elevated.

And in just five short months, we launched with a big bang. The corporate marketing team collaborated with us to create a Community Space at our global user conference where we promoted the new community, got users excited about the changes, and reengaged.

The first year was a huge success.

- More than 26,000 users visited and engaged monthly, 2x our original goal.
- All posts are answered within SLA, and 85% of posts led to an online conversation.
- Ticket deflection has resulted in nearly £300,000 support costs being offset.
- Crowdsourced ideation resulted in 400 submissions; 100 progressed to the product review board and 20 community-sourced ideas have been released into product.

In addition to achieving these goals, we also introduced gamification, a user-driven content blog, specialty-focused user groups, and have continued to invest in improving the experience by listening to our members through our always-on community feedback loops.

This story proves that an active community is a win-win. It enables users to help other users, drives ticket deflection lowering support costs, and gives users a mechanism to have their voice heard by the company. Plus, when we as organizations work to build customer-centric cultures, we collectively deliver an experience that is a competitive differentiator, thereby positively impacting the company's financial performance.

ADVOCATE TYPES

Laura Ramos of Forrester Research states there are four different types of advocates,[21] and I completely agree.

1. **Educators:** The first are educators. These are advocates who like to share knowledge, tips, and/or tricks. They're outgoing, enthusiastic, and enjoy helping others. In my opinion, educators are perfect champions. They teach others how to use your solution effectively, and I think you should aim to find as many educators as possible.

2. **Validators:** Next up, there are validators. These advocates are well spoken, fair, and balanced. They're trustworthy, credible people, and they're willing to go on record for something they feel strongly about. They are perfect for CABs.

3. **Status Seekers:** Status seekers are ambitious but honest people. They want to progress their careers and are typically very good at public speaking. Usually, these types of advocates have extensive networks, both on LinkedIn and in the real world, and progress through the advocate maturity map quickly. They want to promote their personal brand internally and externally and want to be seen as experts. Status seekers are great for events.

4. **Collaborators:** The fourth advocate type is a collaborator. These are people who are influential and are willing to give their time and their energy to something helpful. They tend to focus on long-term strategy and understand it to be a key necessity. Typically, senior employees fall in the collaborators channel and do very well on CABs.

---

21 Laura Ramos, "Build an Effective Customer Advocacy Program by Knowing the Four Advocate Types," Forrester Research, June 11, 2020, https://go.forrester.com/blogs/build-an-effective-customer-advocacy-program-by-knowing-the-four-advocate-types/.

WHO'S ON FIRST? WHO SHOULD OWN ADVOCACY?

From what I have seen, most of the time, marketing owns advocacy, which, when you think about it, makes sense on the surface. "We need to do a video testimonial for the website." If it's related to video or the website, most people immediately think of marketing as an example.

But remember the billion-dollar company I mentioned earlier in the chapter? The one with 47 case studies? Their customer advocacy program is owned by marketing, and this is a trend that I see quite often as marketing is primarily focused on acquisition. But advocacy is not just about acquisition; it's about so much more. Maybe it's time to challenge the status quo.

I believe that customer advocacy should be owned by customer success because CSMs work with the customers day in and day out. They know who the advocates are, and they can best identify and nurture them.

Customer marketing still plays a fundamental role in capturing conversations with your customers and realizing value, and they are the ideal distribution engine. But I don't think they should be the manufacturer. Customer success should partner with customer marketing because marketing knows the target audience—a stipulation customer success leaders should understand.

Marketing is the face of the brand to prospects, and customer success is the face of the brand to customers. However, both teams should be actively involved in each other's work in this area.

The point I'm trying to make is that when it comes to advocacy, there are many similarities between marketing and customer success, but customer success should be the department that owns the process because they are the face of the brand to the customer. They are best suited to find advocates and extract value. Instead of marketing reaching out to customer success, asking for an advocate to do a case study on a particular product, it should be customer success saying, "Hey, marketing. I have 27 case studies I need to build. Can you help me?"

When you understand the difference between the two departments and realize the distinct roles each group plays, your collaboration will enable you to massively amplify your advocacy program.

HOW CAN OUR TOOLBOX HELP?

Are you ready to start talking about how the tools can help with customer advocacy? Then let's do it.

MOMENTS OF TRUTH

When you think about all the events that happen during the business cycle—great implementation, easy onboarding, proactive customer success—these are all moments of truth that provide an opportunity to identify an advocate.

Your ears should perk up when a customer says, "This is the best support we've ever had. No other vendors do it like you."

As customer success professionals, we hear these kinds of compliments all the time, and when we do, it's an opportunity to say, "Would you like to write an online testimonial about it?" Just ask. Nine times out of ten, a customer will say yes. Typically, the testimonial is very much a win-win. As a vendor, we get positive advocacy. The *customer* gets to say how smart and cool you are by achieving certain wins and outcomes. The individual gets recognition in the broader market (perhaps a future employer will approach them), and their brand gets to showcase how smart they are and craft a narrative that speaks to their market messaging.

By understanding moments of truth, you can drive advocacy.

PLAYBOOKS

There are a few playbooks you can create to help you with advocacy. You should have a playbook on how to identify an advocate, as well as one on how to nurture them and then get them to engage. You can also draft a playbook on how to build case studies and how to capture references. What's the process for getting a customer to write a blog article or attend an event? Write a playbook to establish one.

CUSTOMER HEALTH

When it comes to customer health, advocates typically score high on at least one of the metrics we should focus on—product usage, business outcomes, service utilization, customer feedback, and support. For the Advocacy Pillar, business outcomes is the most useful. When you can quantify, demonstrate, and give your customers great outcomes, it's a prime time to find a whole bunch of new advocates. It could be a stakeholder, influencer, or user. Whoever is touching that product and experiencing those outcomes is a potential advocate.

CUSTOMER RISK

Sentiment risk is the most prominent customer risk in the Advocacy Pillar. High sentiment can equal a high advocacy probability. It doesn't guarantee it, but if someone is bullish about you and your solution, you can typically get these customers to the nurture phase pretty easily.

Inversely, negative sentiment will lower your advocacy probability, so you have to constantly monitor it. You can do this by looking at NPS or CSAT scores. You can also look for poor sentiment on a product or services survey. If your champions or end users are expressing frustration or indicate a deteriorating customer relationship, it's likely you have a sentiment issue and thus, a problem.

CUSTOMER SUCCESS PLAN

The most prominent element of the Customer Success Plan for the Advocacy Pillar is the advocate maturity map. We've already talked about this, but to remind you, your map should include the advocates you've targeted, nurtured, engaged, and promoted.

SEGMENTATION

Segmentation is used heavily in advocacy. Let's take a look at CABs, for example. When determining how to create them, think about how you can segment them based on products, verticals, geography, product, annual spend, and so forth. Segmenting your CAB is a great use of the tool.

Think about the different types of advocates discussed earlier. Some prefer testimonials, and others thrive at live events. Identifying your advocate type will help you determine how they can best promote your solution.

QBRS AND EBRS

These metrics really shine in the next pillar on strategic advisors, but you can discuss advocacy during QBRs and EBRs. "I've noticed we've moved the needle here. We had a slow start, but we worked together and made some fantastic progress. Would you be willing to share that experience?"

QBRs and EBRs are two of the primary tools you can use to get your customers to agree to testimonials and referrals because they can act as a springboard. If everything is going well, you can use that to start a conversation with one of the executives in attendance. If things aren't going so well, you can use that to your advantage, too. In the *next* QBR and/or EBR, once you have proven your ability to turn things around, you now have a customer who is even *more likely* to agree to be an evangelist.

VOICE OF THE CUSTOMER

As advocacy is literally the voice of the customer, I'm guessing you already know why this is important. Although voice of the customer is generally referring to taking customer feedback and relaying it back to your own organization, helping a positive/insightful customer's voice to be amplified to the market is just as important.

CUSTOMER DELIGHT

If we think about HubSpot's definition of customer delight again, we start to understand that exceeding the customer's expectations and delivering a great customer experience with our product/brand to improve loyalty is what the Advocacy Pillar really reflects. So think of it this way: as we've explored in this book already, delivering business value to the customer is the ultimate customer delight. So every customer we achieve this with must become an advocate.

TIPS AND TRICKS FOR ADVOCACY

It's time for some advocacy tips and tricks. I've got four for you.

1. HIGH ADOPTION

If your customer is fully using your product (or using the full number of hours or bandwidth, etc.) and leveraging its capabilities, that's a good sign. When a customer is all in, the likelihood they'll become an advocate is high. Go find them.

2. NET PROMOTER SCORE (NPS)

I've referenced NPS several times throughout this book, and if I'm being frank, I'm not really a big fan of it in general. (I could write a whole chapter about it, but I'll save you the time. Instead, read how I really feel about it in a shortened tirade below.) I *do*, however, think NPS is helpful for identifying advocates, and that's about it.

NPS is a simple metric many companies use. Traditionally, it asks, "How likely are you to recommend our business to a friend or colleague?" and gives the respondent a scale from one to ten to choose from. If they select a nine or a ten, they are considered a promoter. If they select a seven or an eight, they're considered passive. Anything six or below is considered a detractor. These are people who will tell others your solution stinks. NPS is great for identifying potential advocates because it identifies promoters. Target your promoters to quickly identify likely advocates.

Be warned, however. It's great for identifying advocates, but that's about all—it certainly isn't the be-all end-all many business leaders make it out to be. NPS measures *perceived* behavior (at a specific point in time), but it doesn't measure *actual* behavior, and more often than not, those numbers don't match up. Humans don't always do what they say they're going to do (shocker!), so putting all your stock into an NPS score because a high percentage of survey takers reported they will recommend your product isn't a good idea because it doesn't mean they actually will. Using NPS to make major business decisions is problematic.

3. TRACKING

Tracking who your referrals are and which customers are referring you will help you understand how much advocacy your company is driving and the impact it's having. For CSMs, a bonus is that tracking advocacy is a great way to boost your performance appraisal. "I nurtured 30 advocates, engaged 20, and got *10* to promote our product." Tracking advocacy is a measurable way to know if you've done a good job.

4. REWARDS

This tip manifests in two ways. First, reward your customers for being advocates. Lucky for you, there are software platforms that allow you to programatize advocacy and reward behavior. You can give your advocates points, gift cards, or any number of fun things. It's definitely something worth taking advantage of. Second, I think you should reward your CSMs. If they get five case studies, for example, they get a bonus or a weekend away (when there's no pandemics around). Maybe it's as simple as they get a hoodie. Whatever the reward is, when you recognize and reward your CSMs, it will reinforce and drive advocacy.

NPS: FRIEND OR FOE?

I have always struggled with the importance a lot of businesses put on NPS. I just don't get it. It's good for identifying advocates like I mentioned, but a lot of business leaders use it to measure the success of their organizations overall. In my opinion, that's a mistake.

The main purpose of NPS is to garner whether a customer is going to recommend your product; however, more often than not, this *perceived* behavior (intent) doesn't line up with *actual* behavior. Customers say they're going to recommend a product, but they aren't actually doing it. Here's a real example: "I hate my bank. I will leave them." Five years later, they're still with the same bank. My intent doesn't match my behavior because it's too much effort to align them.

This is typical of human behavior. It's easy to talk a big game; it's a lot harder to follow that up with real action. This is why I pound my fists on the table (not really, but it sounds nice) every time someone I'm working with emphasizes the importance of NPS in measuring a company's future success. It's way too problematic. Use it for advocacy, and leave it at that!

ACQUIRE CUSTOMERS FOR LITTLE TO NO MONEY

If you find an advocate, someone who is willing to promote your brand, then the customer advocacy program receives their feedback and capitalizes on it. Customer advocacy gives you a competitive advantage. It helps you acquire new customers (for little to no money) and solidify existing ones.

We are almost at the end of our customer success journey. But we have one more pillar to discuss. I know, it's gone by so fast, hasn't it?

CHAPTER 9

PILLAR #7: STRATEGIC ADVISOR

"VALUE PRESCRIBED"

The Seven Customer Success Pillars

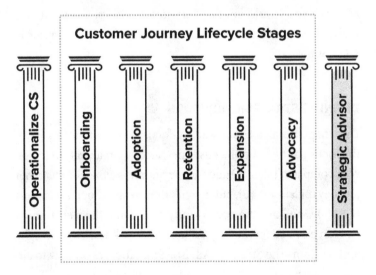

Customer Journey Lifecycle Stages

Operationalize CS · Onboarding · Adoption · Retention · Expansion · Advocacy · Strategic Advisor

www.cspillars.com

What is a strategic advisor? In the real world, what does a strategic advisor look like?

A strategic advisor is not the same as a trusted advisor. Throughout the years, I have seen the majority of the peers I've worked with (I won't say 100% because I don't like absolutes) want their CSMs to be trusted advisors. It's written in their mission statements and on their websites. "We aim to be your trusted advisor."

But shouldn't *all* of your employees be trusted advisors? If I call your support desk, I want to be able to *trust* the advice they are giving me to fix my problem. If I work with marketing on a use case, I want to *trust* they are advising me on industry best practices. The same goes for finance, sales, account management, professional services, you name it. Everyone who works at your company should be a trusted advisor.

Many of you think you need trusted advisors, but what you really need are strategic advisors. That's what this chapter is all about.

DEFINING STRATEGIC ADVISORS

This chapter is also about shifting focus. Throughout this book, the focus has been on the customer success organization inside your company (pillar #1) and the specific steps along the customer journey (pillars #2–#6), but now, it's time to talk about *individuals* (CSMs) who have the opportunity to provide their customers with an elevated level of capability, industry knowledge, insight, and wisdom. The Strategic Advisor Pillar focuses on how to elevate performance and value inside your customer base.

How would *I* define strategic advisor? Like this:

> *A strategic advisor is someone who actively advises organizations on important strategic decisions, in an unbiased fashion, using deep industry knowledge and domain expertise, to deliver the best outcomes through business and digital transformation.*

The first part of the definition—*actively advises organizations on important strategic decisions*—is pretty straightforward. Strategic advisors give advice on big-picture initiatives. They look at where the business, industry, and vertical are headed, anywhere from 6 to 24 months down the line, and guide their customers accordingly. Strategic advisors are proactive and look at the future, which differentiates them from the typical CSM of today.

Sometimes the best solution for our customers means working with other products and services. *Unbiased fashion* means giving your customers the best possible advice to help them drive to value and achieve their desired outcomes. Anyone who works for your company is biased about your products, and strategic advisors are no exception. But the goal is to provide customers with the best possible advice in order for them to be hugely successful, and that means providing unbiased advice.

Using deep industry knowledge and domain expertise is the third part of the definition and refers primarily to education. Strategic advisors need to be educated on the industry and their customer's business nuances. They also need to be educated on the internal products they support and services their organization sells. Combined, this provides the strategic advisor with deep industry knowledge and domain expertise they can leverage to create strategic insights for the future.

Finally, we come to the last part of the definition, *to deliver the best outcomes through business and digital transformation* (by digital transformation, I mean the integration of digital technologies into every area of the business to modify or create new business processes, culture, and customer experiences, to meet changing business and market requirements). Everyone in your customer success organization tries—and wants—to deliver the best outcome, and typically if there's a problem, a CSM will have the training and the skills to jump on it and get it taken care of. However, sometimes the problem may be a symptom of something larger. Strategic advisors are there to think about alternative outcomes to help solve the problem. They're also there to take a step back and look at the entire system. Maybe the problem is manifesting in a completely different department. Strategic advisors take the time to understand bigger challenges so they can come up with solutions to deliver value by transforming how their business is done (processes, culture, or customer experience).

WHY DO WE NEED THEM?

Not only do strategic advisors look at the big picture to help solve overarching issues and challenges, but they also prove to your customers that your organization is knowledgeable about their business and the way they operate. Strategic advisors prove to your customers that you understand their priorities, processes, relationships, and politics. They also bring industry knowledge and in-depth understanding of their company's solutions.

When you give your customer all that strategic advisor gold, it makes it that much harder to switch vendors.

Strategic advisors focus on being valuable assets. Instead of a product or service your company delivers, the value proposition is *you*. This is vital because it makes it more difficult for your customers to leave. If they do, they're also leaving behind their strategic advisor. It doesn't mean a CSM has to be dedicated to the account 365 days a year, but when their expertise is needed, they should be able to show up and transform the customer's business. This means a different approach to managing the CSM's time should be considered as well as their training and enablement.

One last thing before I introduce a new model. I've heard people say CSMs shouldn't always be strategic advisors. Sometimes they are needed for certain tactical challenges, and sometimes it's best they do nothing (just leave the customer alone). Strategic advisors, by their very nature and capability, know when they need to get involved and what they need to do when that happens. Sometimes that's a hands-on strategy, sometimes that's advising on tactical actions, or sometimes that's taking a step back to let the customer do their thing.

NEW MODEL TIME: INTRODUCING THE KSE MODEL™

Strategic advisors are invaluable, but we need a roadmap to get our CSMs there. I've partnered with an industry peer of mine, Shane Anastasi, to co-create a model for developing strategic advisors. It's called the KSE Model, and it comprises the following three components: knowledge, skills, and experience. The model can be applied to any role or function, but for our purposes, we're going to focus on using it for customer success strategic advisors.

KSE™ Model

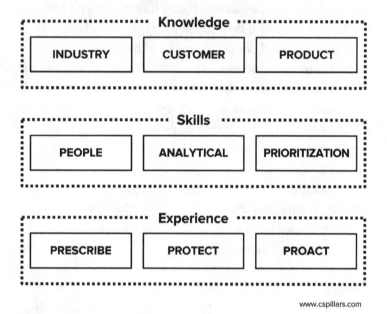

www.cspillars.com

KNOWLEDGE

Knowledge is the first element of the KSE Model, and it too is broken down into three elements:

1. Industry Knowledge

Knowing the industry means understanding industry trends and knowing what's happening in the industry. This means looking at research and trend reports. It means following relevant publications and working with the product marketing team. It means being educated on industry challenges and disruptions.

Are you following influencers on LinkedIn? Are you reading their blog posts and attending their webinars? What about the competitive landscape? Are you looking at your customer's competitors and their differentiated value props?

If you want to be a strategic advisor, you should be. To deliver value, strategic advisors need to fully immerse themselves in the industry and cultivate their industry knowledge.

2. Customer Knowledge

They also need to understand the customer's priorities. This means knowing *more* than values one, two, and three. What is the customer's priority two years from now? How about five? Strategic advisors need to understand these long-term priorities and how their company's products and solutions will drive the customer to those outcomes.

Customer knowledge means understanding relationship maps, too. A relationship map is a hierarchy of all the players managed by the customer success organization. It illustrates who influences whom, who gets along with whom (and who doesn't), who is trying to steal someone else's job, and so forth (usual company stuff). The more a strategic advisor understands what's going on inside these companies, the better they understand what to leverage when trying to sell their strategic vision.

Let's say you're a strategic advisor and a stakeholder within your customer's organization is resistant to your idea. A relationship map will tell you if there's someone in the organization who can influence them. Maybe there's someone they know well and trust because they've worked together before. Maybe they follow each other from company to company. If you can convince this person your idea is sound, they may be able to influence the stakeholder on your behalf.

Customer knowledge means thoroughly understanding the customer's desired outcomes as well. This is part of the CSM's role, but a strategic advisor takes it a step further by understanding an outcome the customer may not fully understand yet.

3. Product Knowledge

Finally, strategic advisors need to have a deep understanding of their company's portfolio of products and solutions. They need to know their solution's features and functionality and familiarize themselves with the company's product roadmaps.

If the company is small (e.g., a ten-person startup), knowing the product inside out should be relatively easy to achieve. But if the company is massive like IBM, understanding all 20,000 of their products and services would be impossible. So what should the strategic advisor do? Work to at least learn all about the solutions their customers are using (in your area of transformation opportunity).

Next, strategic advisors need to understand how their customers apply the products. What are their use cases? If a strategic advisor can uptell and say, "I know you're competing against these other three companies. They've deployed these particular initiatives and these specific processes, and we could actually leapfrog them if you use these two other products of ours." There's nothing better than helping a customer go from number two or three in their industry to number one, but in order to make suggestions like that, strategic advisors need to fully understand their products and the features that will most impact the customer.

Finally, strategic advisors need to understand their product differentiators and what gives them a competitive edge. What are the transformational capabilities of the product? (Start by understanding where transformation has already taken place in the existing customer base, through the use of your company's products and solutions.) What are the product's sticky features? Which will make the customer operationally dependent? How can they be embedded into the customer's workflow? Strategic advisors make sure these differentiators are deployed to maximize the value your customer has the opportunity to obtain.

SKILLS

Knowledge is the first component of the KSE Model, and skills is the second. Every CSM should have a specific set of skills, behaviors, and attitudes. They need to be great communicators and terrific teachers. They need to have incredible time management skills and excel at building relationships. They also need to have grit, tenacity, and confidence. They need to be enthusiastic.

But a strategic advisor has to take it a step further. To do that, there are three skills subcategories we need to focus on.

People Skills

There are really three people skills strategic advisors need to harness in order to deliver the highest possible value to their customers: people, analytical, and prioritization.

1. Assertiveness

The first people skill strategic advisors need to harness is assertiveness. When you're leading a customer to success, you have to have the confidence to say no. You are the expert, both on your product and the industry. Assertiveness is having the confidence to drive your agenda forward to achieve the customer's desired outcome, even if it means pushing back. And guess what? The customer is not always right.

2. Empathy

The second people skill to develop and embody is empathy. Customers want to be heard, understood, and recognized. They want to be validated. Empathy is about listening to a customer's pain points and having them explain why they feel the way they do. If you don't understand what they mean at first (because you don't have the right background), ask questions to find out why the topic is significant to them. You don't need to solve their problem right away; just seek to understand it and the impact it has.

I've worked with companies that have hired specifically for empathy—if the candidate doesn't pass the empathy test, their interview process ends, regardless of the skills (or recommendations) they have. Empathy has become one of the most sought-after, essential skills for employees today, especially in customer success.

3. Relational Intelligence

Finally, strategic advisors need to have relational intelligence. This is the ability to read others quickly and understand their motivations so they can build rapport quickly. This skill is necessary because to align a company with the strategic vision they're painting, they need to get everyone on the same page. Strategic advisors must understand a customer's motivations and drivers.

Analytical Skills

Next, strategic advisors need to fine-tune their analytical skills, specifically data analysis. This skill wasn't even on the radar three years ago because back then, we were all stuck in a dashboard and reporting world. "We give you the information and now you react." But our tools have become more sophisticated since then, and now we have data platforms like Looker and an enterprise data warehouse like Big Query to look at big data and be able to find actionable insights. We have machine learning (ML) and AI and massive parallel processing capabilities, and strategic advisors must be able to understand how to leverage it all.

Internal systems, tools, and processes are going to automate a lot of this for us, but the human component remains priceless. Human intelligence is needed to develop an elevated, strategic understanding of the data to create a vision and determine the next steps. If you're a CSM hoping to develop into a strategic advisor, you have to be comfortable with data. You have to have the analytical skills to mine data and interpret it.

Strategic advisors also must be able to find meaning in the data. What good are data and analysis if you don't understand what it means? There is nothing more rewarding than telling a customer about their business using data they didn't know existed. When a strategic advisor can pinpoint problems, issues, challenges, or opportunities, using data received from the customer, they are elevated in their customer's mind.

Presenting data-driven solutions is also a must-have for strategic advisors. When talking about a potential strategy, it's great to say...

"I wish...I believe...I think...I hope..."

But if you can back your strategy up with data, it becomes tangible, defensible, and real. Including data will certainly enhance your chances of becoming a strategic advisor.

There is one last analytical skill every strategic advisor should have—analytical awareness. That is the ability to deconstruct information into smaller categories in order to draw conclusions and make transformational recommendations. It's new, but it's going to become a major component of customer success.

Prioritization Skills

To round out the skills component, let's talk about prioritization. Strategic advisors need to know how to prioritize their inboxes, their calendars, and their brains. They need to know how to identify what's most urgent and what to work on first.

1. Inboxes

For the majority of us, our inboxes suck up the majority of our time. Email is a killer—it consumes our day. We hope and we pray there will be a product out there that will solve it someday, but we all know these are only pipe dreams. The inbox will forever remain the inbox.

So how do you prioritize it?

I think you should treat your email inbox like you do your physical mailbox. When sorting through my mail at home, I first look for bills and/or checks because it's necessary to pay bills and deposit money. These items are typically urgent, too. Bills have due dates, and I think it goes without saying that we all want to get our money into our accounts as soon as possible.

The next things I look for are items of mail from people who mean something to me, such as family or friends. I also look for correspondence from clubs I belong to. Finally, if I have time, I look through catalogs, brochures, and coupon books (but most of the time, I toss this stuff into the recycling bin). I think you should treat your inbox the same way.

Stephen R. Covey did a great job of illustrating how best to prioritize time in his book *The 7 Habits of Highly Effective People*. In it, he describes four different quadrants, which we can apply to inbox management.

Prioritization Tips

	Urgent	Not Urgent
Important	**I** ACTIVITIES: Crises Pressing problems Deadline-driven	**II** ACTIVITIES: Prevention Relationship building Recreation New Opportunities
Not Important	**III** ACTIVITIES: Interruptions Some phone calls Some mail Some meetings Popular activities	**IV** ACTIVITIES: Trivia Some mail Some phone calls Time wasters Pleasure activities

Important vs. Urgent

- The idea here is that important is different from urgent, but sometimes the two get muddled up in our minds and on our schedules
- Important things are the things that are going to help you achieve the results you're after
- Urgent things are the things that require immediate attention. Items can be either, both, or neither; there is a handy chart in the book that helps you figure out what's what

You should tackle the Quadrant I stuff quickly so you can focus the bulk of your time on Quadrant II activities that actually help you achieve your goals.

Minimize Quadrant III and IV activities.

www.cspillars.com

The first is for high-urgency and high-importance items, such as emergency meetings or last-minute deadlines. Quadrant two is for items that are vital but not urgent. These are times that are going to help both you and your customer achieve your desired outcomes. The third quadrant is for distractions. These are items that are urgent but not vital. For example, if the phone rings while you're working on something, do you answer it? Or if you get a text, do you respond? I do. These are distractions because they divert your attention. Quadrant four is for items that are a waste of time and trivial, such as watching TikTok videos or scrolling through your Instagram feed.

Like I said, we can follow these same principles when prioritizing our inboxes. Focus on emails in quadrant one first and then move on to quadrant two, and so on.

2. Calendars

Strategic advisors also need to prioritize their calendars and make time for connection. What do I mean by that? Customer success activities usually fall into one of three categories—customer support, regular meetings, and relationship.

The first occurs when a customer wants attention. Something is broken or something is wrong. The customer needs information, so the strategic advisor gets pulled in. They support the customer and need to be responsive.

Next up are regular meetings. Typically, all employees have regular meetings with their customers and managers and quarterly company town halls. There are also product roadmap webinars, training sessions, and team meetings.

The third activity, relationship, tends to get ignored. Customer support activities and regular meetings are what we all tend to focus on when organizing our calendars. *I have five hours of meetings today, which means I have three hours to work on my customers' needs.*

But strategic advisors need to focus on relationship, too. This means reaching out to the customers to ask them questions and carving out time for office visits. Strategic advisors can connect with their customers by watching how their employees use their software or service. They can literally shadow employees or even "sit in the chair" for the day to understand the roles that leverage the solution, for example.

I have noticed the relationship element is oftentimes lost because so many of us are wrapped up in the customer's inquiries or busy with too many meetings. Strategic advisors should find time to connect with their customers, even if this means booking in advance.

If you're a strategic advisor and need help figuring out how to carve out more time, take a closer look at those regular meetings that seem to dominate your calendar. For each one of them, you should ask, *Am I fully engaged? Or am I just phoning it in while I work on something else? Is this the best use of my time?*

3. Deep Work

After developing inbox and calendar skills, every strategic advisor should invest in their brain through deep work. Most of us are so busy supporting our customers, knowing our products, and understanding our stakeholders' desired outcomes that we forget to make time for ourselves. Why is this of concern?

I think Covey explains it best—he calls this skill sharpening the saw. It's easier to cut down a field of trees if you stop every once in a while to sharpen your blade. Otherwise, the blade dulls and loses its effectiveness and value. A dull blade simply cannot chop down as many trees as a sharp one.

Many of us think, *I don't have time to stop because I have too many trees to cut down.* But if you stop and take the time to invest in yourself, you will keep your mind crisp and ahead of the curve. Continuous learning will make you more knowledgeable so you can continue to add value to your customer. Otherwise, your value decreases. Good strategic advisors take the time to invest in themselves and sharpen the saw. They make it a priority.

EXPERIENCE

Strategic advisors need in-depth knowledge of their industry, their customers, and their products. They also need experience.

Shane is the world's leading expert on understanding the experience element of the KSE Model (he *did* co-create it with me, after all). He wrote *The Seven Principles of Professional Services* and built a successful company training professional services executives and consultants (http://www.psprinciples.com/). I have adopted his explanation for experience (with his permission of course) as part of the seven pillars because it doesn't matter whether you're a strategic advisor or a professional services consultant—it's paramount for anyone who meets with a customer to nail the experience component of the KSE Model.

There are three elements to experience:

1. Prescribe

Prescribe is how a strategic advisor expresses their experience. It is how they advise or make a recommendation. They are the experts and they *prescribe* how to accomplish something.

Let's say you've been a CSM for three months. You're already more of an expert on your products than your customer because they are implementing your solution for the first time. You have likely already seen three or four different customers go through the process, so you are equipped to *prescribe* the appropriate next steps.

Sometimes customers will push back. "No, thank you. That's not what we're going to do." In those instances, a more successful argument or a different tactic will work, but ultimately, if they don't heed the advice, the consequences need to be prescribed. "If you don't follow my instructions, these are the problems you're likely going to face. I'll need you to sign this agreement stating that any issues with the implementation moving forward are your responsibility and not ours, as you are not following our prescribed approach." This really changes the game. Now you're ready to have a real, honest conversation with the customer.

2. Protect

Strategic advisors also need to have the experience to protect their customers. This means not backing down from uncomfortable conversations because care for the customer and their desired outcomes is paramount.

Protection is about consequence management. When we advise a customer, we're prescribing a process and prescribing an outcome. If the customer chooses a different path and nothing is said to the contrary, this is called implicit acceptance. Basically, by saying nothing, we're accepting the customer's decision and indirectly telling them it's okay. And that is, well, not okay.

When a customer makes a choice that a strategic advisor doesn't agree with, it is the strategic advisor's responsibility to have a difficult conversation and explain the consequence. This is where the assertiveness skill comes in. Maybe the customer has a challenge that needs to be better understood. Maybe they just need to vent. Strategic advisors need to protect their customers and act in their best interests, even if it means protecting them from themselves.

3. Proact

Last, strategic advisors need to proact. They need to lead their customers to success, proactively and with confidence.

CSMs respond to inquiries and incidents. They review results, analyze data, and examine events that have already occurred. CSMs spend a lot of their time reacting.

Strategic advisors, on the other hand, plot the course and look for deviations. They are heavily involved and own the customer Customer Success Plan. They hold firm in their recommendations (because of their experience) and aren't afraid to be assertive. They're prepared to push back and escalate if necessary because they want the customer to have success. A strategic advisor is an elevated layer of capability.

The KSE Model prepares strategic advisors for success with their clients. It's also a great performance tool because it can be used to measure effectiveness and identify areas of growth. "I've got my analytical skills nailed down, but I could work better at protecting the customer." The KSE Model drives improvement and inspires discussion. If you're currently a strategic advisor, it helps you master the skills you need to excel. If you're looking to become one, it tells you everything you need to get started.

KSE™ Model

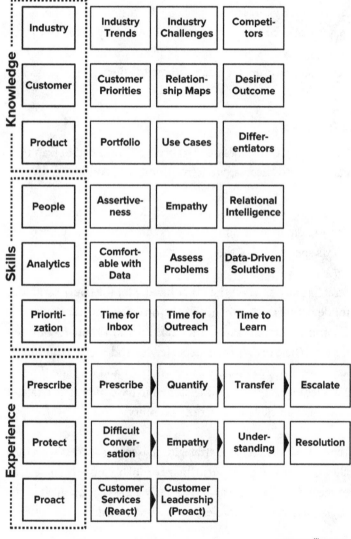

www.cspillars.com

HOW CAN OUR TOOLBOX HELP?

The KSE Model is a specialized tool to help strategic advisors become better at their jobs. We can use the Customer Success Toolbox for help, too.

CUSTOMER RISK

Customer risk is the other tool to focus on in this chapter, specifically noncontrollable risk.

Noncontrollable risks are risks we can't predict, foresee, or plan for. COVID-19 caused every customer in the world to experience a noncontrollable risk—there was no way anyone could have foreseen a global pandemic, let alone planned for one. Yet, when the virus struck, businesses around the world were forced to react. And they had to react quickly.

Noncontrollable risks happen fast and sometimes out of the blue. Laws and regulations change all the time, as do industry standards. Sometimes the risks are due to the macroeconomic environment, such as bankruptcy, acquisitions, or a bear market economy.

We can't control when these things happen to our customers, but we can control how we respond.

For example, you might have received a message along these lines in early 2020: "To help you get through this pandemic, we're going to suspend all renewal charges for the next 90 days. We know it's a financially tough time and in order to get through it, you need the ability to leverage our tools and products. So we're going to make that easy for you."

Strategic advisors help customers in their time of need. Sometimes this means getting creative and figuring out how to appropriately blend the customer's values with the allowances you're authorized to offer. But ultimately, the goal is to help customers succeed in spite of uncontrollable risk.

QBRS AND EBRS

QBRs and EBRs are the perfect time to let your inner strategic advisor come out, especially during the EBR. The ability to articulate industry trends, the customer's desired outcomes that can be attained with your software is table stakes. However, having the ability to understand the longer-term trends, hidden opportunities, and game-changing innovation that your company can bring will help to elevate your status within the customer's eyes.

And don't think that you have to work on all this yourself. Leverage the value and insights teams, transformation officers, or innovation teams within your company to help craft the vision.

TIPS AND TRICKS FOR STRATEGIC ADVISORS

To round out the pillars, I'm going to leave you with some tips and tricks to become an awesome strategic advisor. I've got seven in total.

1. LISTEN TO YOUR CUSTOMERS AND SEEK TO UNDERSTAND THEIR POINT OF VIEW.

Every employee who works directly with the customer should be doing this, but there is a distinct difference between the responsibilities of a CSM and a strategic advisor. CSMs will listen to their customers, take notes, and then act on what they heard. They will then report back to the customer and say, "This is what I've done for you. I've solved the problem and found the answer." Finally, the CSM will ask for input, implement it, and start the process all over again.

Strategic advisors are a bit different. They listen first, but before they take action, they seek clarification. They ask questions to clearly understand everything the customer is trying to communicate. They also repeat what they've heard to the customer. "This is what I heard, and this is what I've interpreted. Can you confirm I've got it right?" Once a strategic advisor knows the information is correct, they then take action and report back. Many customer success professionals miss these crucial two middle steps.

2. BE PROACTIVE. REACH OUT AHEAD OF TIME ABOUT POTENTIAL ISSUES.

Strategic advisors want their customers to have confidence in them. If there is an issue, the worst thing they can do is sit on it until the customer finds out. Strategic advisors should be proactive so their customers know they're at the forefront of information and can be listened to.

3. BE YOUR CUSTOMER'S ADVOCATE.

Strategic advisors do what's best for their customer's business goals and objectives. Sometimes that means being unbiased and recommending another company's product or service either in lieu of or in addition to their own company's solution. Strategic advisors need to advocate for their customers and keep their best interests in mind, and they need to do it as often as they can.

4. EDUCATE YOUR CUSTOMERS CONSISTENTLY.

Strategic advisors share insights and feedback. They work hard to educate their customers on their own businesses and help them identify blind spots. Strategic advisors share their unique viewpoints and keep their customers educated and informed.

5. OVERCOMMUNICATE AS MUCH AS POSSIBLE.

Many people think it's annoying to overcommunicate with their customers, but I think it's essential. Things change constantly, both in business and in life. People change roles. Budgets get cut (or expanded). Goals change. Objectives change. It's an ever-evolving world, so it's crucial for strategic advisors to overcommunicate with their customers in order to align both companies' goals and objectives. "These are the goals we're going to focus on for the next three months. These are the priorities. Do you see any upcoming changes to the business that would impact these goals and objectives?"

6. BUILD RELATIONSHIPS HIGH AND WIDE

At a minimum, every strategic advisor should have a 3 × 3 model when building relationships. They need to have relationships on *three* different levels within the organization *and* with at least *three* of the customer's employees, on each of those *three* different levels.

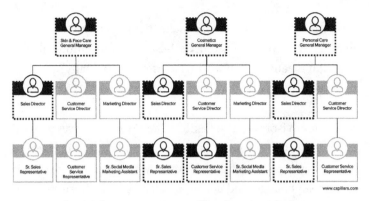

A 3 × 3 relationship is represented by the nine circles.

Key relationships include the stakeholder, a mid-level manager, and a project manager. They also need to understand the relationships within a customer's organization. They should proactively introduce themselves and asked to be introduced. Strategic advisors cast a wide relationship net because the more people they know, the more diverse insights they can gather.

7. FOCUS ON LONG-TERM SUCCESS

Strategic advisors address immediate challenges, but that isn't all they do. The good ones prioritize their time and carve out space to think about their customer's future. They are then very specific in the way they present their vision of the future to their stakeholder. Strategic advisors focus on the long-term success of their customers.

ELEVATE AND CELEBRATE

Strategic advisors are more than just another customer success employee. They are the element that will elevate your customer success organization and make it great. Strategic advisors add a level of experience and authority that not only guide your customers to success but also make them operationally dependent. They keep their customers' best interests in mind, always, even if it means recommending a different company's product or service.

Strategic advisors are also flexible. They keep their eyes focused on their customers' goals (as well as trends in the market) to help mitigate change and advise on how best to accommodate it. Businesses change, and customer success is the business function geared to change along with them.

What does the future of customer success look like? Are you curious?

None of us know what the future will bring (COVID-19 is proof positive of that), and I'm no exception. Where do I think customer success is headed? Here's what I believe...

CHAPTER 10

———

CRYSTAL BALL TIME

THE FUTURE OF CUSTOMER SUCCESS

At the end of 2019, if you had told me there would be a global pandemic that would halt commerce and trade around the world in less than three months, I would have asked if you were feeling okay. COVID-19 hit hard and it hit fast, and it was completely unpredictable.

The future is unpredictable. We have no idea what will happen tomorrow, next month, or next year. We can think about it, create theories around what we *think* might happen, and make plans according to those theories, but at the end of the day, you really don't know what the future holds.

Customer success is the same. I don't know what the future of customer success will look like, but I *do* know it will be different than it is today. I also know that it will have a profound impact on how software companies work in the future.

What that impact looks like, however, I truly cannot say. I have my own ideas based on current trends and how I've seen customer success change in the past, but these are only theories. Only time will tell if my theories come to fruition. I think the future of customer success will impact organizational structure, go-to-market strategies, funding models, talent, and analytics.

WHERE WILL IT LIVE?

The future of customer success begins with finding its rightful place in the organization because it will directly impact the function's effectiveness. Correctly placing customer success within your organization will unleash its full power.

Customer success (or more specifically, the owner of the customer journey) should report directly to the CEO. Currently, I notice a lot of nondigital-native companies develop customer success functions within their organizations under sales, limiting their ability to achieve wild success. This is a mistake (and one of my biggest professional pet peeves). This trend prevents the customer success function from fulfilling its obligation and reaching its true potential.

As I said, you find this structure in larger, traditional companies more than in young, modern ones (or younger companies with digital native leaders). This could be due to a more traditional way of thinking. The leaders of these large, traditional companies are extremely experienced experts in their industries but have little to no experience with the SaaS and cloud-based tech movements. Considering customer success is a function born of those movements, the disconnect is easy to see.

PRE-SUBSCRIPTION ERA MINDSET

This trend isn't happening intentionally—it's happening as

a result of a pre-subscription era mindset that simply isn't as effective in today's subscription-model world. In the pre-subscription era, the head of sales ruled the roost. They were the person responsible for the majority of the company's revenue and was thus a very powerful person in the organization. Back then, all revenue was tied to sales (and a little piece from services or support functions). It didn't matter if it was new customer acquisition, retention, or expansion. Before subscription-based business models, sales got credit for it all.

But all that started to change when the subscription economy arrived. Suddenly, customers no longer needed to pay a massive amount up front. Instead, they were asked to pay monthly. This transactional change also inspired a change in the way customers expected to see value. In the past, it would take years to implement software and drive to adoption. Today, customers expect to see value on day one. If they don't, they will cancel their subscription and go somewhere else.

Land and expand is the motion of increasing sales. Older companies and executives try to shoehorn sales hunters into farmers missing the true value of a customer success organization. It's not about selling more licenses (traditional sales model); it's about exposing value and helping customers achieve their desired outcomes. This comes from customer success management.

And these changes caused business leaders to have to put more emphasis on retention, which if you think back to the very first chapter of this book, was the first wave of customer success. Customer success was born to focus on retention so sales could focus on new customer acquisition.

ORGANIZATIONAL COMPLICATIONS

In the first wave of customer success, when the function was a baby, there were no complications in the way it was structured because no one noticed a problem. But what do you think happened when companies started to grow? What do you think happened when customer success started to own more revenue than sales from retention?

It resulted in a massive complication. "I'm the head of sales or chief revenue officer. I should own all the revenue. Customer success should report to me." Traditionally, sales owned all the revenue, and seeing larger revenue dollars sitting under a different department looked weird—and ruffled a few feathers. But over time, if a business is successful, expansion and retention revenue will increase proportionately faster than new business revenue. It's just math.

Salesforce, for example, renews more than $20 billion in revenue each year, but their new customer acquisition revenue is much smaller than that. They can't sell $20 billion in new revenue annually. Customer success has the job of retaining revenue from customers who have been using the platform for 20 years. It's just easier to retain $20 billion in revenue than it is to newly acquire it.

So it's also no wonder a lot of CEOs place customer success under sales. It makes sense for three reasons.

1. THE ARGUMENT IS COMPELLING.

Sales has traditionally been responsible for all revenue. Customer success is retaining revenue, so tying it to sales makes traditional sense. Moving customer success under sales also simplifies their company's organizational structure.

2. IT LESSENS CONFUSION AROUND EXPANSION.

What do I do with expansion revenue? Does this fall under customer success or new customer acquisition?

The answer, unfortunately, isn't black or white because there are different types of expansion. There is transactional expansion, which is a price increase, additional licenses, add-ons, and so forth. Transactional expansion activities fit squarely inside customer success. Strategic expansion is cross-selling to new departments or selling new products to existing customers. For me, strategic expansion fits better under sales.

3. IT'S EASIER.

When customer success reports into sales, it means there is one fewer direct report the CEO has to be responsible for. It's one fewer person to keep track of. It's easier.

These are the reasons why a lot of company CEOs place customer success under sales, but I'm here to tell you that's all wrong! Customer success should report directly to the CEO (or at least a chief customer officer).

HANDY HINT

If you are approached by an executive recruiter about a head of customer success position, simply ask whom the position reports to. If it's not the CEO (or chief customer officer), politely decline and move on. Your career and the function's success is 100% tied to this organizational structure, and having success under sales will limit your ability to do what's needed for the customers, your team, and your own effectiveness.

Could it work? Sure. But why expend energy fighting against an older business model of thinking when modern thinking CEOs welcome the direct impact of customer success? Seek out those companies.

A DEATH SPIRAL

I'm not alone in this thinking either. Dave Kellogg (he previously worked at Salesforce) wrote an article about this. He claims that when customer success reports into sales, it's detrimental to *both* teams. You want sales to focus on sales. When customer success reports under sales, the sales team gets sucked into account management issues such as renewal challenges and transactional expansion conversations.[22]

The idea seems collaborative, but it's actually destructive. Sales is a really, *really* hard job, and I challenge anyone who thinks otherwise to put themselves in a salesperson's shoes. Try to sell against your competitors and live off your commission check. Sales is hard, and you need your salespeople to focus on it without any distractions. New ARR has to be their metric of success.

Customer success suffers, too. When the function sits inside sales, it forces the customer success team to be support oriented (like it was in the past) rather than growth oriented. Customer success exists today because the old way of doing things needed improvement. It was created to fill in the product gaps. But as you've seen in each of the pillars, customer success has grown into a growth engine. When the customer success team reports under a sales organization, they are pushed into a support role. They aren't empowered to expand business or identify advocates.

---

22 Dave Kellogg, "Should Customer Success Report into the CRO or the CEO?" Kellblog, March 13, 2020, https://kellblog.com/2020/03/13/should-customer-success-report-into-sales-or-the-ceo/.

When a CSM isn't driving value, they are more likely to handle support issues themselves. They want to create value *somewhere*, so they work tirelessly, with restricted resources, until they get the job done. This creates a death spiral. On the other hand, when a CSM is responsible for expansion, they are more likely to behave in a way to help expand an account rather than retain an account.

WHEN YOU DO IT RIGHT

When you build compensation plans and operational models correctly, customer success will flip major expansions over to sales, and sales will flip incidents and insights back to customer success. This means customer success will find sales opportunities and share them with sales, and sales will find areas of improvement and share those insights with customer success. You don't want your farmers competing with your hunters and vice versa, do you?

Another advantage of separating the two is that it creates another professional avenue for your sales professionals. Instead of closing three deals a day, they can have access to 10 to 20 customers with transactional expansion opportunities. Once they learn the ins and outs of how customers operate, they can transition back into a sales role. Keeping the teams separate creates an easy and beneficial way to rotate employees around the company.

Separating your customer success and sales team creates an internal system of checks and balances. Oftentimes, salespeople are tempted to book new business they know won't renew.

"I know you don't have any support people and can't afford this

$200,000 product, but I'm going to help you out. I'll sell it to you at an 80% discount."

The salesperson is motivated by new ARR. If they need $40,000 to get to their number, they're going to make that deal every time. They are incentivized to close new business. We're telling them to do this.

Regardless of the lack of renewal, a smart SaaS company doesn't want that customer's business anyway. They will inevitably be the customer who is always in trouble and always calling support for help. These are the customers that escalate issues and create a lot of noise inside the organization. There is nothing about this situation that's good.

Customer success is measured on gross churn and has a strong incentive to call the sales team out when they make deals like this. "This isn't a smart deal for us. This customer isn't going to renew, and they aren't equipped to manage the product internally. They're going to *cost* us money. We need to pass." Separating the teams creates a natural checks-and-balances system and suddenly you've got two executives at the same level having a conversation about what's best for the company, not what's best for the individual team.

When customer success and sales *each* report to the CEO, the result is absolutely beautiful. Sales can focus on new customer acquisition, something they're really, *really* good at, and customer success can focus on growing customers, its core skill.

GO TO MARKET

The organizational structure of customer success is changing and will continue to change in the future. How we go to market with customer success is going to change, too. It already has. Now, I could write an entire chapter on this subject, but for the sake of brevity, I'm going to keep it quick.

MISSION STATEMENTS

One of the first changes we're going to see is to customer success mission statements. They will start to more clearly define what we do. Here is an example of what a mission statement would look like using the seven pillars:

> *We ensure our customers onboard, adopt, renew, expand, and become advocates through strategic business value delivered with operational discipline.*

EMPLOYEE INVESTMENT

The future of customer success means investing in your people. If you have a platform where technical coding is needed, train and certify your CSMs on the platform. Teach them the best practices on using the application or provide case studies on how to innovate with the product. If you have a CSM on a very large account, train them on the vertical space where the account lives. Like Stephen R. Covey says, "Sharpen the saw."

Your CSMs have the biggest impact on your customer success organization and should be treated as such. Invest, invest, invest in your customer success team. It's time to question the annual budget for employee enablement (it's typically a blanket amount for each employee). These individuals are weapons you can use to expand your revenues and profits at a greater rate than any other person in any other function. (If I haven't convinced you of that up to this point, I've done something horribly wrong!) Why wouldn't you overinvest in that?

MONETIZATION

This isn't really a future activity because this is happening *now, but it's only in its infancy.* The majority of my peers have done a really good job of adding CSMs into paid offerings. The easy way monetization began with customer success was to tie it in with a support revenue product.

"If you upgrade to premium support, you'll get a dedicated CSM with a much smaller portfolio of customers who will be able to spend more time with you."

But we need to get past this real fast. As companies grow and grow, simply adding additional CSMs becomes problematic. Once you add ten new CSMs, you need to add a CSM Manager. These additional costs drive down margins, so you as an organization have to get tighter on your spending.

Some say, "I'm not going to put CSMs on accounts worth less than $200,000. Based on our segmentation strategy, I'm going to move lower-revenue accounts to tech touch."

Technology is getting better, and we as business leaders are getting better about personalized journeys at scale, but in the end, having a *human* who cares about the customer is priceless. However, we're kidding ourselves if we think the company is going to foot the bill for that human connection indefinitely. So we have to figure out other ways to monetize customer success.

The key is success services. I notice when this is discussed broadly inside organizations, the more traditional leaders scoff at it. But when you think about it, all the post-first-sale organizations have monetized. Professional services, education services, support services—why not success services?

Ideally, these success services are outcome based, time bound, business value oriented, and plug gaps that exist in your current customer journey models.

STRATEGIC ADVISOR

As customer success leaders, it's our job to figure out how to monetize customer success. The success services idea above is just one concept. But we should keep pushing to think about customer success in a different way. I think we need someone who has the in-depth industry knowledge and analytical skills of a strategic advisor but is tactical and on the front lines, like a CSM. I think we need a new breed of CSM, and that is exactly what a strategic advisor is all about.

If I'm Walmart and you sell me a product that helps me solve my logistical problems, that's great.

But if you send in a strategic advisor who says, "This is the trend. This is what your competitors are doing, but here's your advantage because you use this technology and you have this retail footprint. Now, if you started using this feature, you would be able to do *this*, which barely exists in the market right now but provides so much value. The secret isn't out yet. You would be leading the pack."

You know what? I would pay extra for that. That feels like an inexpensive way to get strategic advice for my business and a terrific way to monetize customer success.

INCREASED INVESTMENT IN ONBOARDING

Another trend I'm seeing in the customer success world is increased investment in onboarding. If you think about it, a lot of implementation delays are a result of problems that occurred during onboarding. The same goes for risks, poor health scores, and churn, so it's smart that companies are starting to spend more time and money on refining it.

Don't get me wrong, some companies have been doing this for a long time. This isn't a new thing. Jeff Bezos, the Amazon guy (I mentioned him earlier alongside Elon Musk), invested a couple of billion dollars into Montessori education in underserved communities because he believes that stage of life is the most valuable. He said, "Early success compounds over the life of the child." When we invest in that stage, we give them an incredible foundation of knowledge that will help them succeed later on in life.

This same concept is true when you onboard new customers. You are laying the foundation of how they can expect to work with you and see value.

PROACTIVE SUCCESS

Some of the more forward-thinking companies are building out their proactive success capabilities. Customer success has traditionally been reactionary. CSMs respond to problems or analyze health scores. They schedule QBRs and EBRs to talk about things that have already happened. Pretty much everything a CSM does requires a reaction.

Proactive success is about being, well, *proactive*. It means acting on issues before it's too late (if you see something, say something) or introducing new opportunities before the customer has a chance to uncover them without you. It means making accurate predictions and acting on them.

How do we predict the future? By analyzing data from the past, applying ML and AI capabilities to predict the future, and adding human intelligence to present a proactive view of the future. That's the power of data analytics.

THE BOARDROOM

Right now, customer success is just beginning to get the boardroom attention it deserves. Most companies understand the need for a dedicated customer success function because they see the potential business value. I don't think that's the issue. I think the problem is that very few companies have been able to elevate the strategic importance of customer success within their organizations. For the future of customer success, this is an area where we've got to get better. And I hate to say it, but the COVID-19 pandemic accelerated a need for more customer success because the retention of customers, particularly those struggling, became a much larger strategic importance.

Presenting to the board can be tricky, but at the very least, ensure you provide the following in your presentation:

1. Business goals and metrics used to demonstrate impact
2. Head-count investment as it pertains to the coverage model (partnership with go to market and finance)
3. How you are building automation and scale into the delivery model (partnership with finance)
4. Product gaps that your voice of the customer program is

surfacing (a great place to show alignment with product and engineering)

5. Most critical metrics

What are the most critical metrics? I hear you ask. Well, it will really depend on what the company and board prioritize. But I would suggest you always include:

- Team size and coverage model
- Customer base health (GRR)
- Customer sentiment (CSAT, NPS [ugh], customer effort score, etc.)
- Adoption/usage/growth (license consumption, D/MAUs, feature usage, etc.)
- Time to value (speed to achieve value one, for example)
- Advocacy impact (referrals, referred customers)

THE RISE OF THE CHIEF CUSTOMER OFFICER

And who better to lead this customer success function than a Chief Customer Officer (just ask Jeanne Bliss, the author of one of my favorite books, *Chief Customer Officer 2.0*). One of the most important experiences I've had in my professional life was responsibility for the post-first-sales teams of support, services, education, renewals, and customer success as a Chief Customer Officer, more than once. It showed me how out of date and antiquated our organizational models are for the new world of software. We still drive the customer experience model using designs created for a different business environment, and we cling to a traditional siloed approach, to the detriment of customers.

It's why you see conflict over how customer success fits into organizations (sales, services, and marketing all get confused when something they believe they own is now managed by this new organization).

I believe the future will see brave and trailblazing leaders reimagine the design of the post-first-sales world to map to the customer journey, not the internal silos that exist today. Imagine an organization built around the five central customer journey pillars, for example—team for onboarding, adoption, retention, expansion, and advocacy. But rather than use silos to deliver, we use a *combination* of current siloed teams to deliver. So onboarding would be a collection of success, services, and support as one team, not three teams cobbled together.

Redesigning comp plans, metrics of success, and organizational structures would be challenging, but ultimately, I believe this would catapult the customer success journey into the stratosphere.

For today, however, the responsibility of managing these organizational silos into a cohesive customer experience belongs to the Chief Customer Officer.

THOUGHT LEADERSHIP SERIES: JAY NATHAN

*I love to learn, and identifying people who can help me grow is like finding gold. One of those people is **Jay Nathan, Chief Customer Officer at Higher Logic**. Over the years, I've come to highly respect Jay and his determination to bring the customer success community together to collaborate and support each other in our collective pursuit of knowledge and impact. It is for that reason I have asked him to contribute as a thought leader and, in particular, on transformational customer leadership.*

TRANSFORMATIONAL CUSTOMER LEADERSHIP
FOCUS: THE CHIEF CUSTOMER OFFICER

The subscription business model has fundamentally changed the relationship that technology providers have with their customers.

Forever.

Twenty years ago, we sold and delivered products transactionally—find prospects, close deals, move on to the next.

But today, customers expect more, and they have the power to get it. In almost every market imaginable, there is an abundant supply of solutions for every business problem under the sun. It's never been easier and less expensive for entrepreneurs to design and launch a software as a service product.

Not only are the options plentiful, but customers have unprecedented insight into our products and services before they make a purchasing decision. Social media and a proliferation of industry-specific communities have made it easier than ever for buyers to learn about providers before engaging with our marketing and sales teams.

Recent studies have shown that up to 70% of the buying process is complete by the time a prospect engages with a software provider. This means that marketing and sales no longer control the narrative—our customers do.

Given these realities, what is it that will differentiate us in such a crowded and transparent marketplace?

The next decade's competitive advantage will come from our ability to forge meaningful relationships between brands and customers based on the fair exchange of value and outcomes in both directions.

The ultimate win-win proposition.

Although this sounds simple, our companies aren't designed to deliver customer outcomes. We organize into functional silos such as marketing, sales, support, product, engineering, and so on. We build metrics and dashboards to show how efficient each silo is and undertake the yeoman's work of optimization in service of the business.

As we work to optimize each function, some interesting things might begin to happen. Team member frustration increases when trying to get things done across departments. We begin to hear our customers tell us they feel like they are talking with multiple companies when they interact with us. Cancellations begin to increase because not only are customers not reaching their intended goals, but their experiences of interacting with us are ineffective—a terrible confluence of factors.

We can avoid this fate but to do so will require a pivot in both our mindset and operational execution across the business. Instead of optimizing by department, we'll need to prioritize putting the customer back at the center of our business. This will put the focus back on the end-to-end customer journey and utilize outside-in metrics to help us understand how our customers are doing at each stage.

In startups, it is entirely possible for the CEO to lead cross-departmental efforts to achieve this goal. But as the company grows in size and complexity, so does the job of maintaining customer journey alignment.

To succeed, companies will need transformational customer leadership. Leaders who relentlessly seek the voice of the customer and synthesize it for the rest of the organization. People who can lead through influence, who drive initiatives across all functional areas of the business, many of which they do not own.

In addition, these leaders will require business acumen. They know that growth depends heavily on customer expansion and market-place advocacy. They build a quantitative data model that monitors customer and revenue health and a playbook to drive it. Finally, they'll put all of those metrics into context by combining them with qualitative data and stories.

Enter the Chief Customer Officer—a leader, an influencer, a storyteller. Someone who can turn our customers' outcomes into commercial success.

In my consulting work with SaaS companies, I often pressed customer success leaders to think of themselves in this role whether or not they currently possess the title. While managers oversee teams and drive operational efficiencies, transformational customer leaders take the responsibility of championing the voice of the customer. They then use it as a centralizing force internally to give a higher purpose to the work of every team.

Transformational customer leaders help us blur the lines between departmental silos so we can avoid the fate described above. Every company needs transformational customer leadership.

As subscription companies grow, the installed base becomes the largest component of revenue in the business. Although new logo acquisition will always be a key component of growth, its role as the primary source of growth will diminish.

We see it time and again that companies including Salesforce, Zendesk, PagerDuty, and most recently in the S-1 filings for Snowflake, drive huge corporate valuations on the back of high net retention. Achieving metrics requires a coordinated customer journey, aligning a number of key business tasks:

- Identifying the right prospects
- Building the right product
- Leading with value
- Selling honestly and transparently
- Setting the right expectations
- Delivering on the vision sold
- Partnering to drive their outcomes and experiences
- Listening to customer feedback
- Iterating offerings and go-to-market motion

Whether serving small customers or large ones, customer journey execution is an intricately choreographed dance with many participants and moving parts. The Chief Customer Officer uses their considerable influence, operational know-how, and available resources to tie delivery together with the commitments made to customers at the outset.

Adding transformational customer leadership on top of the Seven Pillars of Customer Success covered in this book creates the conditions for successful business outcomes in any market.

HOW ARE YOU FUNDED?

Prominent thought leaders such as McKinsey, Bain, Gartner, Forrester, and Geoffrey Moore, have all talked about the ROI of customer success.

But how do you fund this ROI? How do you account for its costs? How do you classify customer success expenses? Is it cost of goods sold (COGS), or is it sales and marketing (OPEX)? It really comes down to why some companies prioritize gross margin over net income.

And self-funding, at least in part, may be the best way for customer success organizations to avoid the "cost center trap."

When you think about what a CSM does, it isn't clear cut because they wear many hats and work across many different departments. Some of their responsibilities fit squarely in COGS, and some, squarely in OPEX. If you're a very young software company and your CSM is training and helping support because they know the product, that's COGS. But if you're a mature software company and the CSM works with the renewals team and partners with sales on cross-selling opportunities, customer success expenditures can be classified OPEX.

Typically, as companies mature, the customer success function evolves from COGS to OPEX. This is good to understand from a budgeting perspective. Are you likely to receive more budget dollars on the COGS or OPEX line? It depends on the profitability versus efficiency calculus of your organization's leadership and is something you need to understand for the future as you scale your role. How is your funding model going to play into your ability to grow and scale?

Customer success leaders are starting to get savvier in their maneuvering of the financial mechanisms of the organization and when they begin planning for monetization. When you generate revenue, the funding model problem instantly goes away. If you can sell enough to cover the costs of your customer success organization, you transform from a cost center to a true profit-and-loss center.

CUSTOMER SUCCESS HAS GOT TALENT

I want to start this off by saying that I am a huge fan of AI. I think it's going to be key in the advancement of the human race. I don't think AI is bad; I think it's amazing. It's going to change the way we live and breathe and how we manage customer success, so we need to embrace it.

But there's a lot to be said about human intelligence—we can't forget that. CSMs who are bold, creative, strategic, and empathetic perfectly complement AI, robotic process automation, and all sorts of emerging technologies that help us automate and predict. The human connection merges CSMs and trends in AI to create a seamless customer experience that will only get better as technology progresses. Without a human, however, the capabilities are limited (and vice versa).

Think about all those chatbots you struggle with online or the automated phone system that reroutes you so many times you end up pressing zero for an operator furiously until a human picks up. That's what customer success looks *without* the assistance of human intelligence, and I'm telling you, it isn't a place you want to be. Now, with AI *plus* human intelligence, we can have the best of both worlds.

ANALYTICS: THE LIFEBLOOD OF CUSTOMER SUCCESS

Data is the lifeblood of customer success. Insights driven from data analytics help CSMs fix gaps in the experience and move from generalized communication methods to precise, personalized models that partner with other departments and are designed to scale.

In the future of customer success, data and analytics become even more powerful. Today, it's a core skill, when five years ago, it wasn't on anyone's radar. As our customer success organizations continue to progress, leveraging data to empower AI initiatives will become increasingly paramount. This is why analytics platforms like Looker are beginning to augment the traditional customer success platforms where data is necessary for the app to work. With platforms like Looker, the data *is* the app.

And doesn't that make sense? Automation is everywhere you look. From chatbots to mobile and online ordering, AI initiatives are streamlining processes and creating efficiencies. It only makes sense that the future of customer success is analytics.

But ultimately, even with data at the touch of our fingers, the future is unpredictable. No one knew COVID-19 was coming.

Customer success is the same. No one knows what the future of customer success holds, but I think we can all safely say that it will be very different than it is today. Customer success is an ever-changing entity that ebbs and flows with the customer tide, but no matter the changes, one thing I do know for sure: customer success will have a profound impact on the future of SaaS and cloud companies. Just watch.

THOUGHT LEADERSHIP SERIES: ZACH MICHEL

*Next up, **Zach Michel, Head of CS Solutions Global Practices, Google Cloud**. Get used to the name. It's the name of someone who will change how things are done within software companies in the near future (or actually today within my own organization, as Zach leads a key part of it at Google). Zach is like Elon Musk, without the quirkiness, Twitter account, or the billions; he has the special ability to look at challenges and construct solutions no one sees coming. Zach is changing the face of customer success for SaaS solutions at Google. This one is going to be good.*

AMPLIFY YOUR CUSTOMER SUCCESS IMPACT

One thing we know for certain, in this time of rapid technological advancement, is that more and more businesses, workloads, and all things possible are moving to the cloud. The recent COVID-19 pandemic accelerated this shift for many companies. The movement to cloud comes with great improvements, but these new capabilities are often delivered faster than we can take them in. Imagine the tech industry as a herd of bunnies, all working feverishly to produce a bunny that will change the world. The number of bunnies (technologies or features) begins to metastasize at such a rate that it feels impossible to keep up. The bunny you've paid for and so delicately set up becomes obsolete nearly as soon as you think it's ready. The only way to keep up is to continue iterating on your bunny and implementing what's new while moving on from the almost-immediately archaic. To translate this to the world of customer success: the faster we can help customers adapt to the ever-changing environment around them, the more wildly successful they become.

The challenge we face today is the majority of the customer success market is filled with business savants, change management experts, and COOs who dream of getting their hands dirty again. Nobody can deny how pivotal those skillsets are, but we're starting to see that without engineering skills, these savants can't execute the game plan they've so eloquently devised. One common solution is increasing sales engineering head count, dedicating a sales engineer or two to key accounts, and another is adjusting professional services prices to be more affordable. The major pitfall: humans go where the money takes them. Revenue growth incentivizes sales engineering and the utilization of professional services—systems that at their core are nothing without moving on, moving fast, and cutting costs. Before you know it, sales engineers are tied up in prospect accounts, and consultants have more work than they can handle.

So how does one solve this problem? Enter customer success engineering, a group of customer-facing engineers incentivized by overall customer growth. Simply put, customer success engineering focuses on customer outcomes, scalable solutions, and knowledge transmission. Remember the bunny? Customer success engineers (CSEs) would help your bunny be dumbfoundingly cool.

A CSE's time is split nearly evenly across the three pillars: working with customers to achieve their business goals, taking note of common hurdles and frequent requests, and then constructing solutions that sit beside the product for any of your customers to use and resolve their needs. CSEs will morph your bunny from a single solution bunny to a badass rockin' bunny wearing eight-inch platform shoes (I had to fit the word *platform* in there somewhere). The final pillar allows CSEs to truly scale as technical thought leaders, synthesizing the knowledge and best practices they know so well into technical documentation and white papers that help the entire industry move forward.

Of course, nothing is perfect, and there are still risks when bringing a customer success engineerng function into your organization. The good news is, a single mindset can prevent most, if not all, of said risk. That mindset is designing solutions for scale. It sounds cliché when you say it out loud, but it can't be underestimated. One-offs are inevitable, as that's the nature of creating a righteous bunny, but what's important is acknowledging shared fibers that need to be solved more holistically. A team of CSEs who spend a majority of their time providing spot fixes and singular coaching sessions is destined to fail. If CSEs act as an additional tier of troubleshooting, rather than engineering solutions to deflect those support cases altogether, you've found yourself with extraneous support engineers.

Business savants and field-facing engineers, when paired together, are able to provide solutions that enable your customers to adapt to the constant change, ensure visions are technically feasible and eradicate any roadblocks that stand in the way.

CONCLUSION

CUSTOMER SUCCESS THROUGH EMPLOYEE SUCCESS

As I mentioned earlier, my grandparents taught me the tools I needed to survive and find my way back home, and there were definitely a few times I needed them.

But those are tales for another time. More importantly than surviving in the bush (at least I think so), my grandparents taught me the tools to survive in the real world. They cut through the chaotic noise of my childhood and led me down the path to success. I was struggling to find my way in the world, and they were there to guide me.

The same can be said about customer success. There is a lot of noise out there (some of it helpful) and sifting through it is overwhelming. Plus, as a business function, it's still relatively new. How do you know which advice to trust?

Many business leaders are struggling to understand customer success, let alone implement it and scale it. *The Seven Pillars of*

Customer Success cuts through the noise and guides you down a path of clarity and understanding. It teaches you how to drive impactful outcomes for your company (as well as your customers), regardless of size, maturity, or industry.

HERE ARE THE CLIFFSNOTES

Now that you have read this book, you're ready to implement pillar #1 and operationalize customer success. You have all the tools you need—you now know how to write playbooks and create Customer Success Plans . You know how to recognize moments of truth and how to measure customer health. You know how to best utilize QBRs and EBRs and why segmentation is valuable.

You also know how to successfully navigate the second pillar and onboard your customers, define value one, and *proactively guide them to achieve value one as quickly as possible.* Creating an onboarding strategy and making it easy is now possible.

The difference between onboarding and adoption, pillar #3, is clear now, too. Adoption is *achieving operational dependence while simultaneously providing business value,* and you now know it's a crucial step in retention. If the customer doesn't adopt your solution, do you still think they'll stay?

The fourth pillar, customer retention, is the *carefully orchestrated process whereby the customer chooses to extend their relationship with you.* Retention has always been the main focus of customer success, but hopefully, now you understand exactly what happens when you don't retain a customer (other than simply losing revenue) and how that loss impacts the entire organization.

You also know the impact expansion (pillar #5) has. You know expansion occurs when *a customer finds value in your solution and grants you the opportunity to increase that value.* You also know the tools needed to develop a killer expansion strategy.

Pillar #6, advocacy, is well known now to you, too. Customer advocacy is a *competitive advantage for your company because it assists in the acquisition of new logos and solidifies existing customers through a multitude of assets and programs,* which you now have access to.

And last but certainly not least, you now know the importance of strategic advisors (pillar #7). A strategic advisor is someone who *actively advises organizations on important strategic decisions in an unbiased fashion, using deep industry knowledge and domain expertise, to deliver the best outcomes through business and digital transformations.* You know a strategic advisor is not the same as a trusted advisor, and you know having one will elevate your company's standing with your customers.

ARE YOUR PILLARS OPTIMIZED?

We've established that by reading this book, you know how to operationalize customer success.

Okay, so now what?

Take this framework and spread it out across your organization. Look at all the tools and figure out which components already exist. Maybe you already have a few playbooks built around adoption. Maybe you're using QBRs and EBRs effectively. Maybe you've already identified the stakeholders. Whatever it is, write it down.

Next, you should examine and evaluate your organization from the perspective of each pillar. Are they all optimized? Is there something from this book you can use to augment and enhance them? Looking at what you already have is the easiest place to start. Ask yourself, *what do I have right now and how can I optimize them so they're the best they can be?*

After that, you can start to figure out what you're missing. Maybe you have a low retention rate and an even lower expansion rate. Maybe your customer success function rolls up under sales and you're not maximizing its full potential. Find the gaps and then put together a strategic game plan that will determine how you fill them.

For example, if you discover you aren't measuring customer health properly (or measuring it at all), put a plan in place to get that process started. Determine the data you need to calculate the appropriate metrics, figure out how long it will take to gather it, and then build a playbook around how to measure it. Just remember to keep in mind the weighting methodologies we discussed. Otherwise, your customer health score won't make any sense.

The future is completely unpredictable and out of our control. Just like COVID-19, it's an uncontrollable risk. However, when it comes to customer success, there are a few things we can predict somewhat with certainty.

Customer success is here to stay, and how it looks in the future of your organization is entirely up to you. But I will tell you this, if you follow the pillars and take the steps outlined in this book, you're off to a really good start.

In fact, I challenge you to take it a step further. After you're done reading, pass it on to someone inside your organization who would benefit from reading it.

Customer Success Pillars Framework

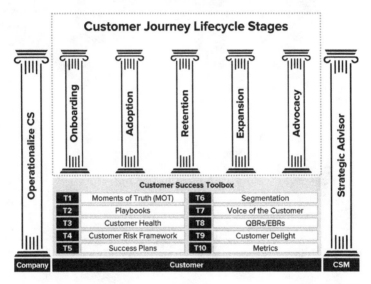

Customer Journey Lifecycle Stages

Operationalize CS | Onboarding | Adoption | Retention | Expansion | Advocacy | Strategic Advisor

Customer Success Toolbox

T1	Moments of Truth (MOT)	T6	Segmentation
T2	Playbooks	T7	Voice of the Customer
T3	Customer Health	T8	QBRs/EBRs
T4	Customer Risk Framework	T9	Customer Delight
T5	Success Plans	T10	Metrics

Company | Customer | CSM

www.cspillars.com

Pillar #1
Operationalizing Customer Success
- The CS Toolbox has ten tools to implement Moments of Truth, Customer Success Plans, Playbooks, Risk Framework, Health Score, Segmentation, Voice of the Customer, QBRs/EBRs, Customer delight, and Metrics
- Moments of Truth are triggers for playbooks that help us operationalize success
- Playbooks are personal activity lists that help us repeat success within an account

Pillar #2
Onboarding
- Value 1 is the first and fastest business value you can demonstrate to the customer after they sign their contract
- It is business value expressed as improvement in revenue, margin, and customers' or employee satisfaction
- The customer experience goal is to make it EASY

Pillar #3
Adoption
- Without adoption there is no renewal
- We must achieve operational dependance and demonstrate business value
- Identifying and engaging stakeholders is key
- Change Management is an essential component that is ongoing, not just at the start of the implementation

Pillar #4
Retention
- Losing a customer has larger ramifications than just lost revenue (lost upsell, lost insights, competitors stronger)
- The goal is to create a stable environment with NO surprises at renewal time
- Customer Success Plan is the tool used to track progress, "license" consumption, if key features are being used, and more

Pillar #5
Expansion
- The CSQL is the way CSMs can visibly demonstrate direct impact to revenue and internal teams
- Using Up-telling, we create Upsell and Cross-sell opportunities
- Expansion strategy includes identifying priorities and improvement areas and then translating that into customer stories

Pillar #6
Advocacy
- Customer Advocacy is good for Competitive advantage, accelerating deal cycles, retention, expansion, and insights
- Deploy assets and Programs to maximise advocacy conversion
- The Advocacy Maturity Map helps identify where advocates are in their contribution to our company

Pillar #7
Strategic Advisor

Knowledge	• Industry: Trends, Challenges, Competitors	• Customer: Priorities, Relationship Maps, Desired Outcomes	• Product: Portfolio, Use Cases, Differentiators
Skills	• People: Assertiveness, Empathy, Relational Intelligence	• Analytics: Data, Assess Problems, Provide Data Driven Solution	• Prioritization: Inbox, Calendar, Make Time to Learn
Experience	• Prescriptive: Prescribe, Quantify, Transfer Risk, Escalate	• Protect: Difficult Conversations, Empathy, Understanding, Resolution	• Proact: Be Proactive, Build Success Plans, Lead the Customer to Outcomes

www.cspillars.com

BONUS TRACK

PILLAR #1.5: PREBOARDING

There may be another pillar of customer success. Of course, admitting that would require me to change the title of the book and that's just, well, a hassle. Also, I'm not 100% convinced the world is ready for pillar #1.5.

What is pillar #1.5? It's the presale, or as I like to call it, the preboarding period of the customer's journey. But it is hard to apply the term *customer* to a prospect because they are not, in fact, a customer. Should prospects then be considered in customer success strategy?

Where it gets interesting is the line between prospects and customers is so blurred now. In the cloud-based subscription economy, where freemium and free trials are common, at what point do we determine when a company is a prospect or a customer?

If a company is using a freemium model, free trial, or proof of concept, are they really a customer? They *are* using the product. The days of having to pay to be classified as a customer may be well behind us.

At Looker, the award-winning Department of Customer Love (customer support) treats prospects and trial companies no different from paying customers. With an average response time of 23 seconds, more than 90% of support tickets resolved during the first contact, and a 98% customer satisfaction rating, not many trial customers get this kind of support. This awesome team of "chatters" helps convert trial customers to *paying* customers every day.

So why not deploy customer success to trial customers, too? Why not think of a freemium or trial prospect as a customer and thus provide them with the same success services paying customers receive (and don't say it's about resources because customer success at scale can equally be applied to customers or prospects)?

We talk about the handoff from sales to success post deal close, but we never question why there should be a handoff in the first place? Why isn't customer success part of the sales process?

Here at Google, I recently saw a great thank-you note from the sales executive to the CSM on the account for their help closing the deal. The customer had many concerns about the deployment, adoption, and long-term value of their investment, and the CSM was able to tell the customer journey story in a way that made the customer feel extremely comfortable with moving forward.

Bam!

Customer success brings the credibility and expertise to differentiate a software solution when it counts—during the presale. And once a customer signs, they already know their CSM, and the CSM already understands value one and has relationships with key stakeholders right out of the gate. This is a great example of pillar #1.5.

So look out for the next edition of this book; it just may include pillar #1.5.

ACKNOWLEDGMENTS

Having an idea and turning it into a book is even harder than it sounds and more rewarding than I could have ever imagined. But being able to get to this point took a lot of inspiration and support.

The primary inspiration came from my closest friend, Shane Anastasi. After he successfully published *his* business book, *The Seven Principles of Professional Services,* he was the spark that ignited the desire within me to write my own. In addition to being the catalyst for this journey, he has also been a part of it in a big way. Pretty safe to say that without his encouragement and involvement, this book never would have come to fruition. Thanks, mate, for your guidance, advice, and most of all, your friendship. And I have to give a shout out to Andy Olsen, who was the OG book Author from the AWS Production team (long before Amazon used that acronym)!

I'd also like to take this opportunity to say I'm eternally grateful to my grandmother, Janet (and my grandad who is no longer with us—miss you!), who endured raising me during my most difficult years. Both of my grandparents taught me manners, respect, a strong work ethic, public speaking, and many more valuable skills than I can count. I couldn't have made it this far without you! And thank you to Mum for bringing me into this world and always giving me unconditional love.

To Tom Hogan, who took a chance on a 29-year-old kid from Australia and gave me my first executive leadership role while at Vignette. He saw a kid motivated to learn, grow, and succeed here in America. He mentored and guided me in ways that have helped me throughout my career (including two more opportunities to work with him over the last two decades). Enjoy your retirement, Tom. You earned it!

My transition into the software industry was as exciting as it was daunting. But none of my subsequent successes would have been possible without some key people along the way. The most impactful of those people being Chris Vidotto. Through his patience and generous friendship, he, along with Rod Walkenhorst, enabled me to make the move into the software industry while teaching me *how* to teach. Chris and his wife, Jeynelle, provided me with a ton of support and encouragement needed during some tough times in my life and were always there when I needed them. Thank you, Chris, for everything you did to help me succeed in the world of software. You are someone I have and will continue to admire throughout my life.

A special shout-out to the software OGs—PeopleSoft, Vignette, Lombardi, HP, Lifesize, Genesys, Salesforce, Kony, and Looker teams! I look back on all those experiences and there are too many people to name who have impacted me well beyond my time with those companies. But I do have to send shout-outs to:

Fiona, Lash, Rod, Kylie, Vicky, Svet, Ian, Paul, Gav, Keith, Hager,

Nora, Staci, Eunice, Kev, Xina, Gaynor, Jeanne, Staci, and the man who made work fun—Michael Hutney! William, Martin, Tricia, Thom, Franz, Ramesh, Madan, Mahesh, Sukie, Alexandra, Brigitta, Vijay, Neelesh, and my cricket buddy Craig Perkins. Alan, Lucy, Jason, Joe, Megan, Alise, Colin, Casey, Sandy, Kevin, Sarah, Jim, Whitney, Dave, and the most interesting man alive, Simon Dudley. Josephine, Julie, Lucy, Andy, Scott, Tiff, Mariko, Atul, John, Maria, and the inspirer himself, Shane-o. Tom, Nate, Todd, Carlos, Dave, Kathy, Amy, Garima, Cem, Ajay, Jess, John, Nag, Kapil, Frank, Matt, Ed, Laura, Paul, Somna, Bruce, Saravanan, Jeffery, Mike, Jean, Mary, Tanmay, Marcel, Burley, Kevin, Paul, James, Claude, Raj, Gina, and the cleverest man I know, Bill Bodin! Margaret, Zach, Lambert, Lloyd, Frank, Brian, Tricia, JR, Razzak, Troy, Kennan, Lucas, Teresa, Jenny, Vicki, Eric, Ryan, Eanna, Shoji-san, and the inspiration to stretch my wings, Nick Caldwell, and way too many more people to thank!

The world needs people who are willing to lead and develop others, and I wouldn't be where I am today without the leadership and *mentorship* of so many. So thank you to those who have shared their insights, time, and *experiences* with me:

- Llyod Tabb, for teaching me what building a real company culture looks like. "Great software is an act of empathy" will stay with me forever.
- Lambert Billet (and Jason Smith), for not giving up and selling me on making the move to Looker—it changed my life and my family's life forever. And a special thanks to Lambert, for providing guidance and support. Thank you for being my champion.
- Maria Martinez while I was at Salesforce, for teaching me what true customer success is and what the importance of operational capability in a leadership role really means.

- Madan Gadde, for showing me what a great people leader looks like and that nice guys *can* win.
- Anand Eswaran, for teaching me: "You're not as good as your numbers, and you're not as bad as your numbers." It's a super-valuable perspective I've have now because of you.
- Toby Cappello, for a short but impactful leadership experience and ongoing support of my career.
- Special thanks to two incredible leaders, Staci Scatterwhie and Jeanne Urich, from early in my management career when I moved to the US. Professional, patient, funny, and empathetic, these two leaders helped me find my management voice early in my career.
- Keith Sheridan, for teaching me the power of coffee. Although I don't drink the stuff, having a "coffee" with colleagues and peers is an essential piece of corporate success.
- To two more (Austin, Texas) CEOs, Rod Favaron and Craig Malloy, for showing me how to build a company from literally nothing.
- Kylie Hammond, for making it possible to get to the United States. Your support meant I could realize my dream of living in the States and having the career I have now.
- A HUGE thanks to Craig Mason, for being my first "real" boss in my career and making it pretty much impossible for any other manager to beat it. And to Ross Bradley for always thinking of solutions when there didn't appear to be any.

There is a group of people I'd like to highlight in particular. These are the OG thought leaders and teachers who, over the years, have helped accelerate my learning in the field. Without their generosity and sharing their time, experiences, and ideas, my customer success journey would have been much slower and more painful.

- Nick Mehta, the first and continuous leader I follow and rely on for all things CS.
- Dan Steinman, the person I look to when thinking about the future of CS.
- Paul Philp, probably the best resource (plus the Amity blogs) for understanding how to apply CS theory to practice.
- Jeanne Bliss, helped me in my first CCO role and through her book *Chief Customer Officer 2.0* to understand how CS fits into a larger post-first-sale ecosystem.
- Irit Eizips, for constantly bringing CS talent together and talking about relevant and timely topics for immediate application through CSM practice.
- Lincoln Murphy, for his no-nonsense approach to CS. Even though we don't always agree, he has incredible insight I always learn from.
- Jay Nathan, for showing me how sharing knowledge helps all of us and the CS profession gain new heights.
- Nils Vinje, his constant push for evolving his understanding of the practical application of the CS profession.

There are so many more people I have learned from, and if you are sharing your experiences with the CS world, keep doing it. The more knowledge we can share, the better our profession will become.

Finally, to all the leaders who directly contributed to the book via the thought leadership sections—an extra special thank-you!

A special callout to the AIP group (formally Peak Teams): Matt, Ryan, Marky, Tab, Rex, Morgan, and others. And the man who started it all, Shane Toohey—a fantastically talented individual (can someone say seven summits!), businessperson, family man, and personal idol of mine. His guidance (from leading global organizations to reminding me to put away my phone when I'm with my kids), *wisdom*, and insights are always incredibly valuable.

And to the two people who believed in *The Seven Pillars of Customer Success* so strongly, they rolled it out across more than 60 countries to transform their customer success organization (the largest deployment of training so far for the seven pillars curriculum)—Danny and Zinnia. I hope that training and certifying hundreds of CSMs on this content will forever change your company's ability to succeed now and in the future!

Getting a book to market is just a crazy, daunting process. I'm forever indebted to Emily Anderson, Rikki Jump, Rachael Brandenburg, Cristina Ricci, Mikey Kershisnik, and Rosalia Rodriguez for their ongoing support bringing my book to life. And to Lisa Caskey (#YOUROCK!), without whom this whole thing would not have been possible—you are my Scribe for life! It is because of all these people's efforts and encouragement that I have a legacy to pass on to my family, where one didn't exist before.

To my wife, Kristi, who sustained me in ways I never knew I needed. Your understanding and patience are unfathomable. I will make sure I work every day to earn a place by your side. To my girls, Peyton and Blayke, for making this whole process that much harder and more motivating than I thought possible. And of course to Bella, for being my best (four-legged) friend, who kept me company all those late writing nights.

Finally, to everyone who reads this book—thank you. The purpose of writing a book is so people can read it and learn something impactful, so I really *do* hope you find at least one nugget of knowledge or one new idea that sparks something great for your career and your organization now and in the future!

ABOUT THE AUTHOR

WAYNE MCCULLOCH is a customer success leader at Google Cloud, across the entire SaaS portfolio of products. Bringing insight to his industry with more than 25 years of experience in various customer-focused roles and as a Top 100 Customer Success Strategist (as voted by the global customer success community), Wayne is one of the world's leading customer success experts.

Prior to joining Google, Wayne began his software career at PeopleSoft and then accepted the role of VP and GM of worldwide education services at Vignette. He was an SVP in the customer success group at Salesforce and then EVP and Chief Customer Officer at Kony, Inc, and a similar role at Looker. Wayne is a keynote speaker and the recipient of multiple industry awards.

For access to Wayne's *The Seven Pillars of Customer Success* training and certification program, visit www.cspillars.com.

CPSIA information can be obtained
at www.ICGtesting.com
Printed in the USA
BVHW031502150322
631521BV00013B/960/J